PROTECTING
DIANA

A BODYGUARD'S STORY

LEE SANSUM

WITH HOWARD LINSKEY

DIVERSION
BOOKS

Diversion Books
A division of Diversion Publishing Corp.
www.diversionbooks.com

For more information, email info@diversionbooks.com
First Diversion Books edition August 2022
Trade Paperback ISBN: 9781635767919
eBook ISBN: 9781635768206

First published as *The Bodyguard* in Great Britain in 2022
by Seven Dials, an imprint of The Orion Publishing Group Ltd.
1 3 5 7 9 10 8 6 4 2

Library of Congress cataloging-in-publication data is available on file.

All photos reprinted by permission of Seven Dials,
an imprint of The Orion Publishing Group Ltd.

PROTECTING
DIANA

To Kate, my beautiful soul mate. You saved me and changed my life, just as you have changed many other lives for the better. I survived the difficult times to come back to you. This book is dedicated to you and my wonderful children: Chamane, Janine, Damon, Theodore, Sebastian and Blake.

∞

For all my brothers and sisters, past and present, who have stood shoulder to shoulder to fight the good fight: thank you. Without you, I would not be here to enjoy my wonderful life or ever to have the opportunity to set down my story in this book.

I am with you and will watch over you wherever you go, and I will bring you back to this land.

Genesis 28:15

CONTENTS

CONTENTS

PROTECTING
DIANA

TREVOR REES-JONES

Trevor was the lucky one. Everyone said that, and I suppose they were right. Trevor Rees-Jones was the sole survivor of the most notorious car crash in history: a horrific accident in Paris, on August 31, 1997, that claimed the lives of the driver, Henri Paul; our boss's son, Dodi Fayed; and the most famous woman in the world, Princess Diana. It sent shock waves around the world, causing a huge outpouring of grief for "the People's Princess," and it changed my life, too, completely.

It could have been me in that car instead of my friend, if my name had been on the roster to be their bodyguard that weekend. I might have been killed or horribly injured like poor Trevor. The shock of the accident, the loss of Dodi and the death of a woman I had got to know, like and admire led me to take stock of my situation. For the first time, I started to really question what I wanted to do with the rest of my life. I had worked for Dodi's father, Mohamed Al-Fayed, for several years, was Diana's bodyguard in St. Tropez just a month earlier and had already signed up to join Diana and Dodi in America, where we had been told they were planning to resettle. Diana had been happy on that holiday but I had seen her in tears, too, when she learned of the murder of her friend Gianni Versace. She confided in me her own fears that she might one day be assassinated.

It was my job to protect Diana, to keep her from harm and shield her from the constant hounding of the paparazzi who would soon be blamed, in part, for her death. The role of elite bodyguard was one I had grown into gradually and was an unlikely position for a northern working-class lad, and former football hooligan no less, to find himself in. I was thirty-five years old and had reached this point slowly and steadily, thanks to expertise picked up in the military police, during undercover work in Northern Ireland at the height of the Troubles and through intensive martial arts training—I eventually became an eighth dan and there aren't many of us around. Later, I would go on to open the most successful martial arts school of its kind in the UK. This thriving business was eventually wrecked by the economic crash, forcing me to earn a living once more by risking my life, this time in the war zones of Somalia and Libya, where I was nearly killed on a number of occasions.

But if there was a single turning point in my life, when events caused me to divert from one path and choose a very different one, it was that crash in Paris, when the world was forced to come to terms with the loss of a much-loved princess and my own future was thrown into doubt, my plans for America ended.

As I waited to meet my old mate Trevor again, for the first time since the crash, I knew he would still be in a bad way. He wanted to see Dodi's grave so he could pay his respects and I hoped this meant that he was getting better. He had spent ten days in a coma following the crash, while we anxiously awaited news of his condition, not knowing if he was going to pull through. Every bone in Trevor's face was broken by the impact. Surgeons had to rebuild it from old photos, using 150 pieces of titanium. They took part of the back of his skull to rebuild his cheekbones. His nose and jaw were so badly damaged that his face was completely flat. You can see that in the X-rays. His surgeon said he had never seen anyone survive such terrible injuries.

So, yes, as the sole survivor of the crash, Trevor Rees-Jones *was* lucky—but he didn't look it when I saw him that day. The poor bloke was a mess and the sight that greeted me when he got out of the car was a shocking one. I filled up with tears, which I had to hide because I didn't want him to know how bad he looked, though I suspect he already realized. He was hunched over and had probably lost three stones in weight. His face was in such a state that you would not have known it was Trevor. The guy could hardly speak and was slurring his words. It didn't help that he was probably on strong meds for the pain and to help with his recovery. I can't remember what I said to him. I probably fell back on the usual dark, squaddie humor that always seemed to help when a situation was truly terrible, though that wouldn't have lasted long. He was here for a reason and I was there to help my mate get to Dodi's grave. I knew this was a big moment for him. I had brought a golf buggy round to the front of the Al-Fayed house. I helped Trevor into it and drove him out to the grave, which was in a beautiful part of the grounds. Straight away, I realized that every bump was going right through him, causing Trevor more pain, so I had to drive very slowly.

When we finally got to the graveside, there were people working on the site, finishing the mausoleum that Mohamed Al-Fayed had built to memorialize his son. I asked them to leave so I could bring Trevor to the graveside. It was obvious he would not be able to get out of the golf buggy without my help, so I bent low, put my hands under him and lifted that big man up and out of there like he was a kid, then I helped him to walk slowly to the grave.

I knew Trevor was a tough bloke who could take it, but he was clearly in a lot of pain and I questioned the wisdom of doing this because it was obviously taking a lot out of a seriously injured man.

"Trevor," I said, "are you sure?"

But he insisted on going through with it.

"I am *doing* this," he said firmly. He was twenty-nine at the time of the accident and had been strong and fit. Now he was in such a bad way that it was like helping an old man. I had to support him the whole time and I was very aware that when we got there, things might become even worse if the grief hit him.

We finally made it and stood together silently at the graveside for a while, both of us thinking our own thoughts. The marble gravestone had the single word "Dodi" carved on it. Sometimes the light would shine down and make it look like "Dodi" was two words not one: "Do" and "Di" appearing to be in different shades. I wasn't the only member of the security team to have noticed that.

Like everyone else, I was desperate to know the truth about what had happened that night and how Diana and Dodi could possibly have been killed. Trevor was perhaps the only man alive who might know the truth so, in the end, I had to ask him.

"Mate," I said, "what was the score in Paris? What happened?"

"I can't remember," he said. "I'm telling you now, I honestly cannot remember and I wish I could." He told me his last memory was of leaving the Ritz Hotel before climbing into that car and I believed him.

Then he said simply, "I hate it."

He meant he hated not knowing. It seemed that the only person to witness the final moments of Diana and Dodi up close was just as much in the dark about the events of that night as everybody else.

Conspiracy theorists think Trevor's amnesia is convenient but I can assure you that it wasn't convenient for him and they didn't see the awful damage he suffered in the crash. No one was more desperate to know what happened than he was. Trevor had massive, traumatic injuries to his face and body. Is it any wonder that his mind and memory were affected too?

I had known Trevor for about three years. We joined Mohamed Al-Fayed's security team just weeks apart in 1995 and got on well from the beginning. He is a really good bloke and a mild guy. If you met Trevor, you would never know he was a former Para, let alone a top bodyguard. It helped that we were very similar. At six foot two, Trevor was even the same height and build as me. On occasion, we would wear each other's suits; for example, if he came into work and found that he was suddenly off somewhere smart at short notice and needed to wear something more formal he'd borrow mine. Trevor had a happy-go-lucky attitude to life but was very professional when it came to his job, just like me.

Princess Diana's long-term personal protection officer Ken Wharfe might well have been the best bodyguard in the world, but in his autobiography he attacked Trevor for his handling of events that night and basically blamed him for Diana's death. He was close to the princess, so I understand how upset he must have been and how tempting it is to blame someone, but I don't agree with him. In the close protection industry, everyone always has their own opinion, particularly when they have the benefit of hindsight. They all have different views on how they would have dealt with a situation, but in the real world, you're working in such a fast-moving environment that you don't always have the luxury of time to sit back and calmly plan your response.

Wharfe said Trevor had not received the necessary training to protect Diana and referred to Al-Fayed's entire team as "bodyguards," using inverted commas in his book to imply we didn't deserve that title, as if we were just muscle. He also said we were "supposedly SAS trained." In fact, there were a number of ex-SAS and -SBS (Special Boat Service) men in our ranks, as well as former Paras, Royal Marines, Special Branch guys, even former MI5 men. Everyone had been expertly trained for the job and we were very good. There were former Royal Military Police (RMP) on our team, too, with loads of close protection experience. They had looked after generals in Iraq and ambassadors in hot spots all over the world. They knew what they were doing.

The security team even had an external policing audit carried out by two of the top Secret Service guys from the States. These Americans ran one of the biggest security firms in the world and they embedded with us for three weeks. At the end, they said we were the most professional team they had ever worked with. During Diana's holiday in St. Tropez, the Royal Protection officers who accompanied the princes William and Harry had enough faith in us and our knowledge to say, "You do what you think is right." And they went along with everything, no problem.

Wharfe also blamed Trevor for letting Diana get in a car with a drunk driver, accepting the widely reported view that Henri Paul had been drinking all day. I don't believe that for one moment because Trevor would not have let a drunk get behind the wheel of the car. There is just no way. The blood tests conducted on Henri Paul that supposedly proved he was drunk were discredited in court eleven years later, during the inquest into Diana's death.

That night, Trevor wasn't treating the paparazzi as the enemy, as Wharfe suggested. He was just trying to give Dodi and Diana a good night, while following our employer's instructions about where to go and when. When Ken Wharfe was looking after the princess, he had the backing of the entire Met Police and all of their resources, which made his life easier. He should perhaps remember that if Diana had been dating a normal bloke, instead of the son of a billionaire, she would not have had any bodyguards with her at all that night. Diana had no close protection of her own following her acrimonious divorce from Prince Charles, a situation that has parallels today with Prince Harry and Meghan Markle's decision to step back from royal duties, which left them without their personal security that had been previously funded by the state, leaving them vulnerable.

When you are the close protection officer to the royals, what you say goes. It is different when you are working for a private individual, who has the final say—it's much harder to refuse them if they want to drive across Paris at midnight. You might not like their decision to go somewhere, you can strongly advise them against it, even resign the next day if you want, but if they have their heart set on doing it, are you really just going to abandon them? Of course not. You are there to protect them and that's what you must do.

Trevor did not do anything wrong that night. I asked him about Henri Paul, and though he cannot remember anything after the moment they left the Ritz Hotel, he did tell me, "I do know he had not been drinking. I would never let anyone drive who was drunk."

"I know you wouldn't, mate," I told him.

Thankfully, Trevor managed to make a good recovery from his terrible injuries and went on to become a security consultant, protecting foreign workers in war zones including Iraq.

The last thing I would say about Trevor to anyone who doubts him is this. I have met a lot of tough, able and professional guys in my time. But I can count on the fingers of one hand the number of men I would trust with the lives of my wife and family and Trevor is one of those very few men.

THE MOST FAMOUS
WOMAN IN THE WORLD

You don't forget the moment when you meet the most famous woman in the world for the first time. It was July 1997 and Dodi Fayed had been dating Princess Diana for a while. Back then, I was spending more time with the Al-Fayed family than mine. I was told we were going to St. Tropez and the big news was that this time the princess was coming too. Wow. Obviously, I was a professional who had to concentrate on the job in hand but at the back of my mind I couldn't help but be aware that the most famous, most photographed and arguably the most beautiful woman in the world was coming on this trip with us and it was now my responsibility to protect her. No pressure there, then.

I had to block that thought out, though. When someone is that famous, people can easily get the wrong idea. They think they know them because they have seen them on TV or in the newspapers but I never wanted to be too familiar with the client. Also, by this stage I had worked for the Al-Fayed family for four years and was used to looking after Hollywood royalty. Personal appearances at Harrods, as well as Dodi Fayed's connections in the film industry as a producer, meant that I had met and protected some very big names indeed. I was determined to take the presence of the princess in stride and keep my mind on my close protection duties.

Al-Fayed owned a home in St. Tropez that has been called a villa, but that really doesn't do it justice. This place was absolutely massive, spread over several levels. The Castle St. Therese has thirty bedrooms, a swimming pool, a beach house and gym, and all of this in one of the most exclusive and expensive places to live in the world. Today, it is valued at £70m.

We were out there for a week or so before the princess eventually joined us. She arrived on the *Jonikal,* Al-Fayed's huge yacht. I first set eyes on Diana as she arrived at the villa on a tender boat. It was one of those little vessels used to shuttle people back and forth from bigger boats. I saw this quite tall and elegant blonde-haired lady coming toward me. She was smartly dressed without being too formal—and beautiful, of course. As the tender boat pulled in, I figured she might need a hand getting out of it, so I ducked down a little and just dropped my shoulder to offer it to her in case she needed to grab it to pull herself up. She didn't need any help but as she got out of the boat she shook my hand and looked at me.

The first words the most famous woman on the planet said to me were, "Wow. More heavies." I just smiled.

Now she was in my care. For the next ten days I would be responsible for the safety of the mother of the heir to the throne.

My first impression of Diana was that she was obviously a beautiful woman but, looking back on it, I think that she was a beautiful person on the inside and that is what made her so special to so many people. I have met journalists and paparazzi over the years who have said to me, "You were Diana's bodyguard?

She was crazy, wasn't she?" I tell them they have no idea about her. Diana was one of the nicest people you could meet. She was lovely, in fact, just a normal person who clearly loved her boys. The poor woman got slagged off for everything she did—even when it was really normal stuff like working out to stay fit, the press gave her grief about that too. It was so unfair.

When we learned that Diana was coming out to join us, we conducted our usual risk assessments. It was pretty clear that we were in uncharted waters here. We had been used to the threats against Al-Fayed and his family but Diana's presence added complexity and a higher level of threat. Her campaign to get rid of land mines worried me most. Even the UK government didn't agree with her on that. She had been a high-profile campaigner in favor of banning them outright and, in January, had even walked along a cleared path through a live minefield in Angola. That extraordinary footage of the princess was shown all over the world, raising a huge level of awareness around the issue, which eventually led to 164 countries signing the Ottawa Treaty, prohibiting the production and use of anti-personnel mines, not long after her death. The people who made the land mines were obviously worried about her campaign, as they were set to lose a lot of money. While the princess was with us, I talked to her about her campaign and she told me about the HALO Trust and how she was helping them to eradicate land mines all over the world. Since then, I have trained their operatives in how to survive in a hostile environment. I even have a picture of me standing next to one of Diana at the HALO Trust.

Following our risk assessment, we decided to step up our anti-surveillance measures. When you are already very vigilant, you can't really be more vigilant but we could send out some people looking for the watchers. There must have been about fifteen of us in total on the team and everyone was needed because it was full-on from the off.

When we were guarding Mohamed Al-Fayed, we were aware that people were watching him constantly and were used to this. We would spot MI5 people during our counter-surveillance drills and why not? It didn't bother us that the security services were watching him. It was just the world we were in. That sort of thing might alarm ordinary people but it didn't bother us at all because they weren't sinister. They were professionals just like us. So we were expecting MI5 and MI6 to be with us when Diana was in the group, whether we were in London or Europe.

Diana was the most famous woman in the world and everyone wanted to get near her. For that reason alone, she was always in danger. Leaving her entirely unprotected, as she was following her divorce, seemed insane to me, as she could have been assassinated or kidnapped by anyone who wanted to make a big statement.

Diana's boys, William and Harry, arrived with two Royal Protection officers, though Diana had no one assigned to look out for her. She only had us because she was dating the son of a billionaire who had a team of bodyguards of his own. I can't help wondering what would have happened if she had been seeing someone normal, who wasn't rich. Also, two police officers are not a lot to cover a holiday involving Diana and both of her sons. If she hadn't been with us, would the authorities really have allowed the heirs to the throne to go on holiday in Europe without top close protection or MI6 constantly watching them to make sure they were safe?

I was busy elsewhere so I didn't see the princes arrive. The first time I saw them was when they came down to the beach. It immediately struck me that they were two very normal boys.

Both were down to earth and friendly, just like their mother, and you could see how much she loved these kids. They weren't shy, they had obviously been around a lot of people and were good at chatting to someone they didn't know, but they weren't arrogant either. Straight away they took to us and we to them. We organized activities for them and took them out on the water to teach them how to use the jet skis. I was on the beach team. Normally, there would have been two of us on the beach but with the princess there we doubled up to four. I'd done this for three years by now. You start with a security sweep then you get the "toys" ready for the family, which included the jet skis. During the sweep, you look for suspicious people or IEDs (improvised explosive devices), even if the risk of that is considered slim. You are watching for anything that is outside the norm, and if you are not looking closely, you won't see it. This could be disturbed earth or something that wasn't there before or isn't where it should be. If a new litter bin suddenly appears, you'd check that out. You are looking for signs that people have been there. Has the grass been trampled down? Is there some fresh mud on that railing over there? These are the telltale signs that someone has been there and done something.

The beach was a private one but in St. Tropez no beach is entirely private, as everyone is allowed to walk across the coastal path, though most people wouldn't choose to do that as the path by Castle St. Therese was too far out of the way unless you had a place nearby. There were some high-profile neighbors. George Michael's villa was nearby and Brigitte Bardot had one there too.

The beach we used was about thirty meters wide with a rocky area behind it and more rocks on either side, so it formed a natural U-shape with a jetty out front. Diana was an early riser so she would be there by about 7:00 a.m., before William and Harry got up. Most days she would come down to the beach and have a chat. I chatted with Diana most mornings. She used to like to sit on the steps by the boathouse and I would be there already, so I would get to talk to her for half an hour or so each day before we took her out on the boats and that's how I got to know her.

The boys would come down to join her on their own. Then the Al-Fayed kids would appear. Karim, at fifteen, was the same age as Prince William, and Omar was ten, a couple of years younger than Harry. Camilla was twelve, the same age as the younger prince, and Jasmine was the oldest at sixteen. They would all still play and hang out together.

The first two days at the villa were great because there were no paparazzi. It was brilliant for Diana and the boys, who could just relax and enjoy themselves for once without intrusion from anyone else. The paps did not know we were there, and in an ideal world it would have stayed that way. We knew it probably wouldn't last, though, and, sure enough, someone must have had a tip-off because the next day we saw them come over the cliff.

There were only two to start with, one photographer and his minder, but they were really aggressive. They wanted to get their exclusive photos of Diana and Dodi and knew how valuable they could be. They were not going to take no for an answer, from us or anyone else.

We tried to turn them around and send them on their way but they wouldn't budge. Worse, they were intent on getting past us and we weren't about to let that happen. My mate was next to me, so it was two against two and I could see things were about to escalate, with the photographer's minder in particular looking like he was going to try and force his way through us.

I told my mate, "We are going to get knocked off this rock face if we don't react. Are you ready?"

He said, "Yes."

Then he hit the minder and dropped him. I took the camera off the photographer and that was that.

The next day, word had got round that Diana was there with Dodi and all of sudden the paparazzi were out in force. It ramped up from that point and they kept hounding us because they were all desperate to get photos of the couple. Diana tried to cooperate with them and did her best to give them what they wanted. She would come out at the start of every day and let them get their shots. She would play ball; they would snap away, getting what they had supposedly come for, then they were supposed to bugger off. That was the deal but they never did. Instead, they stuck around all day because they knew the kind of photos newspapers really wanted. Staged pictures of the family enjoying a holiday were one thing but they would only get the big money for photos others didn't have. They wanted candid, voyeuristic shots of Diana and Dodi kissing or messing around together.

They liked unusual photos and I ended up in one of them. There is one of her on the boat when she leans in and looks like she is whispering something to me. They got that picture and wrote stories about it like they knew what she had said even though they were some distance from us. It was ridiculous. I can speak from experience when I say that she never did most of the stuff they claimed she did.

I felt for Diana and I don't know how she coped with it all. The paparazzi would hang around all day and ruin her holiday with their constant intrusion. The newspapers who bought their photographs were cruel too. Diana would allow them to take photos of her at the villa then the papers who bought them would print the pictures with headlines about her "lording it up" on her holidays. Even when she cooperated with them, they wouldn't give her a break. She just could not win.

We did our best to make things as normal for her and the family as possible under the circumstances. Every morning we would have a team meeting to plan the day ahead. If they wanted to go somewhere, a restaurant perhaps, we would work it all out in advance, including how to get them there while shaking off the paps. We knew every street and all of the routes, so we'd plan detours and create diversions using different vehicles to try to throw them off the scent.

They never stopped trying to follow her, though. They would come after her on motorbikes and use boats and even helicopters to try to get pictures of Diana. It was insane and for us it was a headache because anyone could have been hiding inside the crowd of paparazzi and that made it harder for us to spot a threat.

William and Harry were fifteen and twelve years old then. They wanted to play on the beach so we were down there every day with them, while fifty boats floated just a few yards out, filled with photographers watching them the whole time through zoom lenses. Even the little cruise ships from St. Tropez got in on the act and cashed in. They usually carried normal holidaymakers but when they learned that Diana was at the Al-Fayed villa, they laid on extra boats so they could take everyone out to see "Lady Di" as they insisted on calling her, even though she hadn't been known by that name in the UK since she got married, let alone divorced. You would hear them calling it out from the boats but it usually came out as "Laddy Dee! Laddy Dee!" which sounded even stranger.

Sometimes there were so many boats out there that we couldn't go out ourselves because it was too crowded and no longer safe. I was the one who had to make that unpopular decision.

The press intrusion was constant and overwhelming for Diana but she usually kept her thoughts to herself unless she was feeling particularly sad or vulnerable. There was one day when I saw her in a different light because she had clearly had a few drinks. I picked her up from the *Jonikal* in a speedboat and brought her back to the villa, which was about a fifteen-minute ride, and she must have been a bit merry because she started singing to herself. It was just daft songs, like nursery rhymes, and I thought to myself, *She's a bit pissed.* She stood right next to me by the wheel and we chatted about all sorts of things: her kids, my kids and her life in England.

The press were the bane of her life everywhere, not just in St. Tropez, and she said to me, "There is nothing I can do in the UK. The papers there attack me no matter what I do." Then she told me, "I want to go to the US and live there so I can get away from it all. At least in America they like me and will leave me alone."

I asked her if the boys would be going there with her. "They would never allow me to do that," she replied. "If I go there, I will probably only be able to see them in their school holidays."

You could tell Diana was a wonderful mother, so loving and attentive to her two boys, but it looked as if she might have to leave them both behind in the UK to escape from the press, who hounded her relentlessly every single day of her life. It was also to free them from all of the attention they got when she was with them. It seemed to me that the majority of people in Britain loved Diana but the establishment and the press were destroying this woman. I felt so sad and annoyed about it all on her behalf.

Finally, after days of them ruining her holiday, she'd had enough. Diana was even concerned she was causing us extra work, which was surprising but she was that kind of person. She genuinely cared about everyone. That day, I could tell she was fuming. Suddenly she announced to us, "Right, I'm going out there now to tell them that I'm off to America for good."

Christ, this was massive. It would be an almighty bombshell and I was alarmed because if we thought the press pack outside was huge now, just for her holiday, it would probably go up tenfold if she gave them a story as big as this one. The place would be swarming with paps, desperate to get pictures of the princess who was about to leave it all behind to run off to America. I glanced at one of the royal policemen who was there to look after the princes and we exchanged looks that told me he was thinking exactly what I was thinking: *Oh shit. It's about to hit the fan, big-style.*

We both watched as she got in the tender, accompanied by one of our lads, and went out to a boat that had been chartered by the *Sun* newspaper, where she spoke to the journalist she called "Fat Fred." I was expecting uproar but, to our intense relief, none came. When she walked back over, I waited till I could have a word with the lad who'd gone with her and asked him, "Did she tell them?"

"No," he said.

"Thank God for that."

HOUNDED

Afugter Princess Diana had been hounded by photographers for days, she told me she had recently been to see the prime minister, Tony Blair, about the press. She had taken her boys with her and asked Blair if he could introduce a privacy bill, to change the law and finally get the paparazzi off their backs. He made it clear to her he was against the bill and that was the end of the matter, as far as he was concerned.

Diana told me she was devastated and had to make a supreme effort not to cry in front of the prime minister. "I waited till I was back in the car," she said, "and I cried then."

It was bitterly ironic that, not long after she told me this, Blair made his famous speech at her funeral where he described her as "the people's princess." I watched that and thought, *Yeah, she might have been, Tony, but she wasn't very keen on you.*

Blair was not the only high-profile politician to disappoint Diana. She was friends with President Bill Clinton and told me she had discussed the anti-mine summit with him. She was confident Clinton was going to help her to ban them outright but, in the end, when that resolution came, he did not vote in favor of it but abstained instead.

When I look back on it now, it's amazing to think that Diana was very seriously considering leaving her country for good because of the damaging effect the press was having on her life. Now, more than twenty years later, one of her own sons has taken the same decision she was on the brink of. Harry has effectively abdicated from his royal duties, left his country and resettled his family in America to keep them away from the paparazzi and the tabloid press he still blames for killing his mother. In his bombshell interview with Oprah Winfrey, in March 2021, Harry revealed that his biggest fear for his family was history repeating itself.

Prince Harry was only twelve years old when I knew him in St. Tropez but he could see how upset his mother was because of the paparazzi. I thought it would be good for him to get a bit of revenge on them and the young prince jumped at the chance. I had been teaching him how to use a jet ski and reminded Harry that when you rode one, a twenty-foot-high jet of water comes flying out of the back as it powers along. I then pointed to the waiting pack of paps that had congregated on a jetty not far from us. I suggested that if he happened to ride his jet ski over to them and turned at the last moment, he might be able to give them a dousing. He needed no further urging.

Harry was delighted and he set off toward the unsuspecting paps who were making his mother's life a misery. He reached them, turned at just the right moment, powered the jet ski back toward me and the jet of water shot out of the back, giving the assembled paparazzi standing on the jetty a thoroughly deserved drenching. It was a brilliant moment and he absolutely loved it.

In 2015, eighteen years after Diana's death, I was working as security advisor for Team Scotland at the Rugby World Cup. I was standing on the red carpet at Twickenham with a former SAS man I'd worked with in Libya. I was asked, "Could you move please, sir?" and in walked another security guy with Prince Harry right behind him. He was wearing a cap and he looked at me as he went by. I didn't say anything, of course. I hadn't seen Harry since that holiday all those years ago but I noticed him do a little double take, as if he might just have recognized me but had no idea who I was.

I spent quite a lot of time with the princes. They were really good kids. William was lovely and Harry was a cheeky, mischievous, naughty little boy who was loads of fun. We used to talk to the boys about the military, particularly when we were all on the *Jonikal.* They were fascinated and would sit on the deck and ask us question after question, which we answered as best we could. Obviously, we wouldn't tell them anything that they shouldn't know at that age, but our group included former Paras, Marines and Special Forces guys and we were all happy to talk to them in general about the forces. I was impressed by the boys' knowledge. They had a great understanding of operations and all of the regiments and it was no surprise to me that both of them took to military life when they served in the forces. Harry famously flew Apache helicopters during the Afghan war.

I had rigged up a punch bag in the garage, so one day, after we were done on the water, I told the princes, "Come on, I'll teach you a bit of kickboxing." When I showed William and Harry how to do it, though, I think they were a little bit in awe from watching me kick that bag so hard and weren't too keen to try it themselves in front of me. Instead, we agreed they might give it a go later.

Some people are surprised when they hear that I had conversations with Diana or chatted to William and Harry. They think that might be a distraction in my job and question how I could be in a state of alert if I was chatting to the principal, but it doesn't work like that. There are basically different levels of bodyguard. On the perimeter of an area being protected, you will see guys standing there not talking to anyone. They'll have earpieces in and they've got that steely-eyed killer look about them. The higher up you go and the closer you get to the principal you are protecting, you become almost like a PA as well as a bodyguard and that's not a bad thing. If you are in need of close protection and the people who want to hurt or kill you take a look at me and think I am your mate, not your bodyguard, then I have done my job. They'll see me dressed casually, standing on a beach next to you talking but might not realize that I am always looking out for you. Then, if they try to attack you, make no mistake, I will open up a can of whoop-ass on them.

It felt like being on holiday with my own children and it didn't interfere with the job because I risk-assess everything to the highest degree with my own kids. I am always asking myself, "Could anything go wrong here?" then I have to put things in place to mitigate the risk. I could still be in the moment with my kids or the princes, while alert to any possible danger. It is the art of looking out and looking in at the same time. There is a Japanese word for this, which translates as "wide eye." You watch the people you are protecting while they are doing something but also position yourself at the ideal point to look at them and still see everything beyond them, using your peripheral vision.

Sometimes, especially in Hollywood, the client will want what I would call "a high-level stance" with very visible security. That's when they hire those enormous, muscle-bound bodyguards to walk alongside them at movie premieres, because it makes them feel better. It gets them more press attention, pampers their egos and probably increases their social media following, but there is a downside. Those guys are big but that doesn't mean they always have the skills to protect you. Image is the least important part of my role, and how I look is way less important than the skills I bring with me. If I am shit at my job but I look the part then you are not secure.

In my mind, there are three levels of security. The first is when a client can feel secure but they are not secure. They've hired close protection but it isn't the kind they actually need. They just don't realize it. Sometimes, a client can feel insecure but they are actually secure; they just don't realize that they are completely covered against an external threat. Ideally, you want them to feel secure because they are actually secure. That's when they've hired the ultimate professional.

The art of it is to avoid trouble if you can. You don't want an incident, and if you have done your job properly you won't get one. If you do get trouble and you hit it head-on then people might die. You need a healthy state of paranoia at a level you can control. It's good to be suspicious but you shouldn't be seeing trouble where there is none. My life consists of one dynamic risk assessment after another. It's a never-ending process. Is it safe? Yes . . . check . . . move on . . . then repeat.

For those who still think Diana was mentally unstable somehow, I can tell you that I spent ten days close to her and she was one of the most balanced people I have ever met. I ought to know. I am trained to spot if someone is unbalanced. It's part of my job. You look for signs that people give off when they are under stress because it means they might be about to do something. If you are going to attack my client, you will probably have spent a long time thinking about it. When you build up to a big thing like that, you will show signs of adrenaline and I look for those signs. You might be sweating, shaking or repeatedly nodding your head. Some people wind their watch up or tap their phone without realizing while waiting to act. I am always looking for something that appears different or plain wrong in someone, so I can be ready to move before they do. It's a skill that comes in handy in any hostile environment, even a pub or bar where someone might be about to hit someone else and most people do not spot these telltale signs or they dismiss them, but they are a giveaway if you know what you are looking for.

Diana wasn't excessively angry or out of control. She was normal and very deliberate. When I spoke to her I usually called her "ma'am," but if the moment felt less formal she was fine if you called her Diana. We talked about all sorts of things, including health and her diet because she knew I was interested in those subjects. She used to ask me about diet and training because I knew quite a bit and was taking courses on fitness and nutrition. She told me about her training, and she kept to the most simple but effective regimes. It was a program I would have written for any female trying to keep fit and included a bit of cardio on a bike or rower, then some high repetition work with weights. The whole thing could be done in half an hour or forty-five minutes. It was nothing heavy. Diana had quite an athletic build and I could imagine she would have been good in the gym.

She had a personal trainer but didn't diet to excess and ate healthily and in moderation. That interested me because most people know what they should be eating but they don't always know how much to eat. Diana was always having to sit down to fancy formal dinners but she would just have a few bites and leave the rest. If people saw her do that, they might think she had bulimia again but she was just trying to stay healthy and not put on too much weight. She was the most scrutinized woman in the world and the newspapers would comment on her shape in photographs, which must have put her under a lot of pressure to stay slim and beautiful.

In St. Tropez, she looked normal and healthy to me. One newspaper even published a photo that made her look curvier and ran it with the headline, "Is she pregnant?" When we saw it, it got us all wondering whether she was or not. I think that is where the rumor started that she might have been carrying Dodi's child, all because of that photo from a shameless newspaper.

Diana didn't really talk about Dodi, except on one occasion when I have to admit I overstepped the mark and got into trouble with the princess. There used to be a nightclub in St. Tropez called the Papagayo, where the rich people all hung out. It was the kind of place where a tiny bottle of beer would cost you thirty quid, even back then. Dodi hired the whole place so he could take Diana dancing there privately. It must have cost him a fortune but they had a great time.

Diana was famously a good dancer. She once danced with John Travolta at the White House and with the dancer Wayne Sleep onstage during a charity gala at the Royal Opera House. But poor Dodi wasn't in the same league as her. Not many people are, of course, but this was particularly noticeable when they danced together on that empty dance floor.

The next morning, we talked for a while and I very politely asked her, "Did you have a good night?" and she replied that she did.

It might have been because we had been joking about other things that morning but, having witnessed the two of them on the dance floor, I couldn't help myself. I said cheekily, "Dodi has got some dance moves."

She gave me a look that instantly showed me I had gone too far and said, "Lee, please don't make me be terse with you."

I instantly apologized. She smiled, a little tensely. I smiled back and, chastened by my telling-off, I made sure I never took the piss out of Dodi's dance moves again.

There was another memorable morning while we were out there, when the *Sun* newspaper printed something that I assumed would be of interest to Diana. They had got hold of a very unflattering photo of Camilla Parker Bowles, who'd had a long-standing affair with Diana's ex, Prince Charles, and is now married to him, of course. Two years earlier, Diana had agreed to a bombshell interview with Martin Bashir on *Panorama* and let her feelings about it be known. "Well, there were three of us in this marriage, so it was a bit crowded," she said, in what was surely the most memorable line of an incredible interview.

The *Sun* had put a photo of Camilla Parker Bowles on its front page next to one of Diana in St. Tropez looking beautiful, along with a disparaging headline saying that Charles has "Given Up This for This."

"Have you seen what's on the front page of the *Sun?*" I asked.

"Yes," she said calmly. "I've seen it."

"Interesting," I said.

"Well," Diana replied simply, "it's his choice."

MURDERED

During her holiday, Diana received some shocking news. Her friend, the fashion designer Gianni Versace, had been murdered. He was shot at point-blank range outside his home in Miami Beach.

That morning, the security team were having breakfast when we heard the news that Versace had been killed. Details were scarce to begin with but we learned he had been shot twice by the killer, who ran from the scene. At first glance, it looked to us like it could have been a professional hit.

That day, I ended up on the *Jonikal*. There was always a cabin there for the security team to use and I was looking for it because it had been moved and, at first, I couldn't find it. I was near the back of the boat when I walked round the corner and almost bumped into Diana. When she turned, we were face-to-face and she was only about a foot away from me. Diana was in tears and looked very distressed.

"I'm sorry," I said. "Are you okay?"

Under normal circumstances, when someone looks that distraught you would automatically want to put your arms round them to comfort them and that's what my instinct was telling me to do. Diana really looked like she could have done with someone to offer her a hug just then but of course I couldn't do that. She was the princess and I was her bodyguard, so I could not cross that line, ever, even if she might have wanted me to. I really felt for her but I was also thinking, *Fucking hell, the last thing I want is for Dodi or Mohamed Al-Fayed to come round the corner and see me with my arms around her.* I could also imagine what would have happened if I had done that for a split second and the paps got a long-range shot of it. They would have made a massive story out of a fleeting moment.

I had to stand back to move out of her way, then I deliberately looked out of the window while she composed herself.

"You've heard about my friend Versace?" she asked and I said that I had. Then she said, "What do you think?" It was clear she was asking me about my professional view on the killing.

"I don't know," I admitted but I echoed the thoughts of all of the security team that morning: "It does sound like it might have been a professional job."

Then she said something that always stayed with me.

"Do you think they'll do that to me?" She was shaking and it was clear from her tone that she really thought that *they* might, whoever *they* might be.

I spent some time reassuring her that no one was going to try to kill her and she was safe with us but she definitely thought there was a risk that one day she might be assassinated.

This conversation went on for some time until I thought there was no real point in continuing and that it would be better for us both if we stopped. I made an excuse, telling her that I had to get going as I had things to do. Before I left, I asked her if she would be okay and she assured me that she would. I left Diana and went straight to the head of hospitality and asked her to go and check on the princess to see if she was alright or if she needed anything.

Later, we discovered that Versace's killer was not a professional hit man but a crazed spree killer called Andrew Cunanan. He was delusional and thought he had a close friendship with Versace, even though the designer's family insist they never met. Cunanan killed himself eight days after he shot Versace. The murder might not have been as sinister as we first imagined but there was no doubt Diana was genuinely frightened that the same thing might one day happen to her.

When Diana and the boys were ready to leave St. Tropez, we took them to Nice on the yacht. I was on the *Jonikal* that day and they were all in good spirits, having drinks and a final meal then saying their farewells to everyone.

Before we took them to the airport so they could fly home, I was chatting to Prince Harry on the top deck. He suddenly got a gleam in his eye, then said, "Lee, would you dare jump off this boat?"

I assumed he meant would I do that if it were absolutely necessary, so I said, "If I had to, yes."

"Would you not be frightened?" he asked me. It was a bloody big yacht and a fair drop from its highest point into the water. I assured him I would not be frightened and his eyes widened. The boy clearly had a plan.

"Would you jump off it now? Would you not be scared?"

"I *could* jump off it now," I explained but I hoped he realized I wasn't planning to do it just for a laugh. "And I wouldn't be scared . . . but I'm not going to, obviously."

Harry then asked me, "How much would you do it for, then?"

The prince was clearly trying to coax me or bribe me into a dare, to see if I really was daft enough to chuck myself off the top deck of a superyacht.

"I dunno," I said, quickly trying to think of an amount that wasn't entirely ludicrous but might be enough to put off a little boy, even one with royal blood. "Two hundred quid," I said, hoping that would be an end to it.

He heard that and off he went.

Prince Harry wasn't daft. He didn't go to his mum. He went straight to his billionaire host instead. "Mohamed, can I please have two hundred pounds? Lee is going to jump off the boat."

I didn't hear my employer's reply but moments later I did hear a very familiar voice. It was Diana, shouting up from the lower deck. "Lee, are you really going to jump off the yacht?"

"No," I replied firmly but that wasn't the end of it.

Next thing, I heard Diana's voice again and this time she called, "We've got your two hundred pounds!"

Shit, I thought. *I suppose I'd better do it, then.* A bet's a bet, after all, and this one was by royal command, from an actual princess.

So I jumped off the boat, hit the water with a big splash and they were all delighted, especially young Harry.

When I climbed out of the sea, dripping wet, they were all laughing at me but they didn't forget my money and I got my two hundred pounds. You might imagine that Mohamed Al-Fayed wasn't impressed by my antics but far from it. He loved his security team and was happy to enjoy a daft stunt like that one, particularly if it pleased and impressed his guests. Thankfully, I always had a change of clothes with me, so I could dry off and put some new gear on before they left for the airport.

We said our goodbyes on the boat and Diana included every-one in that, the security team too. The princess had nicknames for all of us and, for some reason, mine was Rambo, though I never found out why and I can promise that I never wore a bandana. Diana called one of the other lads "Shirts" because he was color-blind, which meant some of his fashion choices were a disaster. So much so, his wife had to put numbers on his clothes so he could match them properly. A pair of shorts might have a number one on them and he could then pair them with a shirt that had the same number on it. Without this system, he didn't have a clue. One day, he put his clothes in the washing machine and all of the numbers came off in the wash. From that day on, he was a fashion victim and that was why Diana christened him Shirts. He came down one day in a very loud, red, flowery shirt with green shorts and brown shoes and I said, "Mate, what the bloody hell are you wearing?"

Al-Fayed's wife, Heini, didn't usually speak to security, though she did to me on occasion, but watching the princess and the boys chatting to us must have been an eye-opener for her and she seemed to soften that day.

Afterwards, I received a lovely letter from Diana that was signed by her and both of the young princes. She told me she wanted to thank me for taking such good care of them all in St. Tropez. Diana even apologized to me for making my job difficult, because of the press. I was blown away by that. She then assured me that she and her boys had a "magical" time there and that this wouldn't have been possible without my help. I couldn't believe that a woman as famous and in demand as Diana had taken the time to write to me in that way. It showed the empathy she was rightly famous for. Diana was almost always able to put herself in someone else's shoes and it is one of the reasons why she was so highly regarded. Diana signed off with her warmest possible thanks. I still have that letter and will always treasure it.

I think Diana genuinely cared for everyone. She left me with such a positive final impression that I put my name in the hat to go out to the States to look after them there. Dodi and Diana had made plans to look for a place to live in the same complex and our head of security was asking for volunteers to work as their close protection. We understood we were going out there to look after both of them and this was fed down to us from the top, so it was legit and we knew we had to be ahead of the game. I volunteered because it was an interesting job, but I also wanted to be involved in looking after the princess again because she was such a wonderful woman. I was living on my own at the time and my kids were with my ex-wife. The rotation was to be one month on and one month off back in the UK so, if anything, I would see more of them this way.

I said my goodbyes to the princess and her boys. I assumed my immediate future was sorted and I would see them all again soon, but within a month Diana and Dodi were dead.

LIKE A DEATH IN THE FAMILY

When the St. Tropez holiday was finally over, we were all absolutely knackered. It had been a full-on experience, involving eighteen-hour days. I now wanted and badly needed a rest. Then we were told that Dodi and Diana would be heading for a three-day break in Paris soon and would need security. None of us were keen to volunteer as we were worn out. In the end, we decided that the only fair way to decide who went with them was to draw lots.

Trevor Rees-Jones was already going to Paris because he was Dodi's man, but he needed someone to look after the princess. One of our number, Kez Wingfield, had been off the detail during the St. Tropez trip with a heavy cold and he had been put into quarantine, but the rest of us all drew straws in the ops room to see who would be accompanying Trevor to Paris. I pulled a match and it was a long one. An ex-SAS man called John got the short match. He took one look at it and said, "Well, I guess we all know what this means . . . Kez will be going to Paris."

No one argued with him. It seemed fair enough, since Kez had missed most of the St. Tropez shifts due to his cold. He was recovered by now and we needed rest more than he did. So Kez might not have pulled out that short straw himself but he would be the one going to Paris, while I got a couple of weeks off.

Nearly everyone can remember where they were when they heard the devastating news from Paris, and I am no exception. I had a big barbecue at the house that evening. I remember it was around midnight when everyone went home and I decided to wash all the dishes, which I don't normally do, so I was still awake when I got a call from the ops room. They told me to be on standby and that I might need to come in. When I asked them why, I was told, "There's been an accident in Paris. Dodi and Trevor were both in the car and so was Diana. They are all in a bad way." I couldn't believe what I was hearing. It was awful and a huge shock.

I was in touch with the guys from the ops room throughout the night, getting regular updates on the situation. I found out Dodi had died well before it was announced on the TV and knew the princess was in a bad way. Eventually, we all learned the truth: the princess was dead and I was devastated. I had gotten to know Diana just a month earlier and really liked her. I was planning to go to the US with her and Dodi and now they were both gone. Her two young sons had lost a mother they loved and who adored them. My boss, Mohamed, had lost his son. Dodi's stepmother, brothers and sisters would all be grief-stricken. It was terrible and I felt completely helpless.

The only way I can describe it now is to say that it was as if a member of my own family had died. I knew the Al-Fayed family so well and could imagine their feelings. I really felt for Diana too. I may have only spent ten days with her, but it was recent and fresh in my mind and we had shared a lot of stuff. I assumed she and Dodi would be a big part of my life going forward but it was not meant to be.

If that weren't bad enough, we were also all worried about Trevor. I spoke to the ops room on a daily basis and they were getting almost hourly updates on him. We knew he was badly hurt and it was clear he might not make it. Mohamed Al-Fayed got him the best care and protection possible, which I fully expected from him. We all knew he would. Being part of his security team was one of the only jobs I ever worked where I knew that if I got killed or badly injured while looking after his family, my family would have been looked after forever. That enabled me to do my job without ever having to worry about it.

I drove back down to Oxted to the Al-Fayed family home, to join up with my team and get back to work. I could have taken the train but I needed the solitude this time. It almost felt like going back to my own family. I felt so bad for them all, and I was grieving too.

ACCIDENT OR ASSASSINATION?

I don't think there will ever be an end to the speculation surrounding the crash in Paris that night in August 1997. Opinion will almost certainly always be divided between those who think it was a tragic accident and others who believe Diana was murdered by sinister members of the security services.

My employer, Mohamed Al-Fayed, grief-stricken at the death of his son, was convinced that Diana and Dodi had been deliberately targeted for assassination, but why would the British government or the royal family want Diana dead? Charles and the princess were already divorced. He was free to move on with his life and so was she.

But if it was just an accident, then how can we account for some of the strange things that happened that night or explain the actions taken by the authorities afterwards, which provide almost overwhelming evidence of a cover-up of some kind? Is it possible that members of our security services *were* involved in or at least witnessed the accident but their presence has been completely erased from the official version of events?

The men who went into the Pont de l'Alma tunnel on high-powered motorbikes around the same time as the Mercedes were never traced. They simply disappeared, which seems incredibly unlikely in a modern capital city with extensive CCTV footage.

We had seen men on machines like those before. In St. Tropez, we used a decoy car to block a narrow road while Diana and Dodi went on ahead. The paparazzi were frustrated because they couldn't follow but they didn't hang about. Instead, they went off looking for other routes. The men that stayed to confront us were a different breed. There were two of us blocking their way and we were asked, "Are you going to let us pass, lads?"

"You ain't coming past," I told them, ready for a confrontation.

There was a standoff, while they must have considered taking us on. I can tell you now that from their manner, demeanor, the way they spoke and carried themselves and even the clothes they wore, they were ex-military. How did I know? I just did. One of them even called me "mucker," meaning "mate." Only the military uses this term when speaking to another military person. They were evaluating us to see if we meant what we said, and when they realized they wouldn't get by, they got back on their high-powered motorbikes and rode off.

If you think it impossible that Princess Diana was under surveillance from our security services at the time, then let me ask this question: Can you imagine a scenario where the prime minister contacts the head of MI6 and asks him where Princess Diana is and he replies that he doesn't know? Diana was the mother of the heir to the throne. They would have had eyes on her all of the time. Imagine if she had been targeted by terrorists, kidnapped by criminals or simply compromised by being in the wrong place with the wrong people at the wrong time. No way would the authorities have allowed that to happen. Diana was under surveillance for her own protection but also so that everyone knew where she was at all times, which was surely a matter of national security.

On a counter-surveillance drive near the Al-Fayed home in Oxted, just before we went out to St. Tropez, my colleague Martin spotted a 14 Company (DET—Special Reconnaissance Unit) guy on the route on a building site. I didn't believe Martin at first. I even said, "No way there is a DET guy here."

Martin was adamant. "I'm telling you, I lived three doors down from him in Hereford."

We went back and saw the bloke again and Martin confirmed it was the man he knew from his time serving with the SAS. We were generally followed by MI5 and this was the first time we had seen a Special Forces guy near Oxted.

We thought, *They've upped their game now.*

A witness driving a car traveling in front of the Mercedes in Paris that night told the inquest that he saw a high-powered motorbike overtake the car just seconds before the crash. Another witness traveling in the opposite direction saw a second motorbike swerve to avoid smoke and wreckage then carry on out of the tunnel without stopping. The riders of those bikes were never found and that is no coincidence.

I believe that security officers, possibly British or a combined British-French team, following Diana may have either inadvertently caused the crash or were in close proximity to the car when it happened. If it were known that MI6 operatives were right by the Mercedes at the critical moment, a lot of people would have blamed them for it and this would have been a huge scandal.

I don't believe for one moment that MI6 arranged to have Diana killed. There was no reason to do it and a car crash is not a reliable way to ensure the death of a target anyway. Trevor was in that car. He survived and eventually recovered. I don't think they were trying to murder Diana but I do believe they were there and that would have been enough to implicate them in her death. Perhaps they inadvertently caused Henri Paul to take evasive action. Maybe all they did was follow Diana's car into that tunnel and watch in horror as the driver lost control of it. Either way, if they were there, covering up their presence at the scene of the crash that killed the most famous woman in the world and mother of the future king would have been crucial. It would have been the only priority from that point onwards and would explain why a different explanation for the crash was badly needed: the theory that Henri Paul was drunk.

The official version was that Paul was three times over the drunk-driving limit and his blood tests proved it, but those samples have now been discredited. At the inquest into Diana's death, it was revealed that the samples had been tampered with and might not have been Paul's blood at all.

The first time the French authorities searched Paul's house, they found nothing more than a bottle of champagne and one bottle of Martini there. When they went back a second time six days later, they suddenly uncovered enough booze to stock a bar. The alcohol that had previously been overlooked included bottles of red wine, vodka, port, bourbon, crème de cassis, pastis and Suze, as well as beer. How could they have possibly missed all of that the first time around? The answer is they couldn't have. It had to have been planted there. The whole thing stank but a scapegoat was needed.

Henri Paul's reputation has been trashed. He was an alcoholic, a drunk who drove too fast into that tunnel and killed the princess, Dodi and himself.

The accident was more likely to have been caused by the actions of other people than alcohol. Something happened inside the Pont de l'Alma tunnel that night that caused Henri Paul to maneuver at the wrong time and the wrong speed. Had he clipped a car carrying innocent people at that point it would have been perfect because there would have been a convenient scapegoat, but there was none.

It can be very noisy in a car when you are moving at speed with excited passengers. With photographers in pursuit, they would have been animated. Paul might have been distracted, constantly looking from left to right or into his rearview mirror while he tried to outrun the paps. That kind of scenario is dangerous unless you are trained for it. Things happen suddenly that don't normally occur and Henri Paul has to react to them, while Trevor and Dodi are calling things out to him. At this point, he would have been under a massive amount of pressure and not used to it, so he might well have acted rashly, carelessly or in some way that could have caused an accident. He was clearly driving too fast; at 65 mph they were more than twice the 31 mph speed limit. Inside the tunnel, something caused him to swerve to the right then hit the wall, the impact sending the car careering back across the two-lane road where it crashed into the stone pillar.

Since the paparazzi were trailing some way behind the speeding Mercedes when it entered the Pont de l'Alma tunnel, something else, or more like *someone* else, probably caused Henri Paul to take evasive action at high speed, which resulted in the crash.

That's my theory and I think it is the only plausible one. Crucially, it accounts for the oddities in the story without endorsing wild conspiracy theories involving Prince Philip "ordering" MI6 to murder Diana to avoid her giving birth to Dodi's baby, which makes no sense at all. But if they didn't murder her, what accounts for all the things that don't make sense?

I believe they were there and they knew how damaging the presence of the Secret Service at the scene of the crash would have been. What's more, I get it; I really do. Whether they fucked up and caused the crash or not, the fact they were even at that spot when it happened *had* to be denied, so a whole different story was spun. Henri Paul was over the limit when he got into that car and that's why he crashed, even though Dodi, Diana and, more inexplicably, Trevor did not notice that he was pissed before they let him drive them at speed through the streets of Paris.

BULLIED

After the funerals, I was asked to go back out to St. Tropez to replace a security guy at the villa whose dad had been taken ill. I went for a month and was the only one there, which gave me plenty of time to think—and I had a lot to think about.

It felt at the time like a turning point in my life and that is exactly what it became. Weeks earlier, I had been in that same villa, planning a new future in America, protecting Princess Diana and Dodi. Now they were both gone and I faced an uncertain future as well as a different life from the one I imagined.

During that quiet month in St. Tropez, I found myself looking backwards as well as forwards. I had come a very long way for a lad who was born into a working-class family in an unpromising corner of the northwest of England. My journey so far had been a dramatic, violent and extremely dangerous one.

I was born in 1962 in Rossendale, Lancashire, in the industrial northwest of England, but to begin with we lived about half an hour away, in a block of flats in Salford. My family are all from the Salford area originally but the Rossendale link goes back to the Second World War, when both my parents were evacuated there. Though they never knew each other as children—they met in a pub that Mum's family ran in Salford years later. I was born in Rossendale because my grandparents ran a pub there, but we moved back to Salford when my dad took a job as a caretaker in the flats where we now lived.

Eventually, they managed to get a house in Rossendale and moved again to be with the rest of the family. We lived on a large estate called Edgeside, which was built on the side of a hill, with cotton mills in the valley down below. The mills provided plenty of jobs for the local community and so, back then, people had a bit of money; there were new cars everywhere and the pubs were full. The mums and dads all worked, so the children played out all day then came home for tea. Your parents wouldn't leave the doors open exactly but they did leave the key hanging on a string so you could pull it out through the letterbox and let yourself in through the front door. It helped that it was a close community, where everyone knew everyone, so the presence of strangers would be immediately noticed. The local pub my grandparents ran was the center of everything and a lot of business was done there too.

But when the cotton mills closed in the sixties and seventies, work dried up and the local economy was hit so badly the place went downhill pretty quickly. I have friends who left school with me who have never worked and that is tragic. Instead of full employment, there is only a subculture of working people with high unemployment around them, as well as a lot of thieving and drug dealing. It's a bad situation to be in and some families have experienced generations of it.

My dad's father, Ted, was really tough. As a kid, I'd be round my grandparents' house sometimes when there was a knock on the door and he'd go off and do something for someone. Basically, he was muscle and was occasionally paid to fix people. He was a very skilled boxer and had been what they called a street boxer during the war, when licensed bouts weren't happening. He was such a good middleweight that at one point he was tipped to be a British champ.

By contrast, my dad was a gentle man and not a fighter, so I guessed it skipped a generation. When my granddad trained him to box, he didn't really take to it. When Dad tried to teach me and my brother years later, we used those old eight-ounce gloves. My brother was taller than me with longer reach, so I would be hit by him more often than not and get hurt. I didn't like that, so my dad stopped our boxing training pretty quickly as he didn't want me to suffer.

At school, I was bullied severely and it was all down to this one particular kid. He was a right nasty bastard who used to beat people up badly. I was quite timid at school and the bullying really affected me but I was too proud to tell anyone about it; instead, I would bunk off school to avoid this guy. He went on to have a successful career, but to me he was a nightmare. The worst moment was in an art class when I was fourteen. I remember he hit me so hard I ducked down and put my head under the table because I was crying and didn't want the girls in the class to see. My pain and humiliation wasn't nearly enough for him though. He started stabbing me in the face under the table with his pen.

It was a relief to finally reach sixteen so I could leave school and get away from him. In 1978, I went to work in a factory and became an apprentice sheet metal worker. It meant I was moving loads of steel around and pretty soon the work bulked me up. I was a big lad anyway, at six foot two, but now I started to add muscle.

One day, I went to a local pub called The Volunteers. The place was always a bit rough and the bouncer in there was notorious for throwing his weight around and picking on people. That day it was my turn and he decided to have a go at me. I hadn't really done anything, just spilled a drink or something very minor, but he used it as an excuse to have a pop. He was known as a bully who would bash people up in the pub and, after my experiences at school, I really didn't like bullies. He kept on at me and I just snapped. I don't know why I did it but I told him, "Okay, let's step outside then."

I was a bit naive and really hoped he would just go away but I had called him out in public in front of everyone, so that wasn't going to happen. The place was packed with young people because there was a disco on and he couldn't back down in front of them. When they realized I had challenged him, everyone took a sudden interest. The whole pub followed us out so they could watch what was going to happen. Here I was, about to have my first proper fight and it was going to be in front of a sizable crowd. At this point I had no experience of fighting apart from being hit by my brother wearing a pair of antique boxing gloves. And I may have bulked up from the factory work, but even so, this bloke was an actual bouncer, a man used to violence, and I was still only sixteen. Basically, I had neither the skills nor the experience to take on someone like him. I don't know what the hell I was thinking.

I expect you can guess how this one went. A young bloke with no idea gets a right pasting from a big hard bouncer; he then goes on to take up martial arts because he was humiliated in front of everyone, right?

Wrong.

Things went very differently. When this bouncer came outside to do me, something flicked inside my head and I went for it. Instead of me getting my arse handed to me, I fought this guy and I nearly killed him. It seemed like every time he went to punch me, I could read it and it was so easy to hit him back. I almost felt superhuman. It was the most exciting feeling ever. Almost every time I hit him, he went down. And I hit him a lot. He got a right hiding. That bouncer ended up on his hands and knees pleading with me, "Don't hit me again."

I had just given this thug a lesson, but that wasn't the best part. That school bully I mentioned, the one who had made my life hell, was in the crowd that day, watching, and he saw me knock that big bloke senseless. I spotted him and as soon as the fight was over, I pointed straight at him and shouted, "You're fucking next, boy!"

He must have shit himself because he quickly said, "I don't want any trouble, Lee."

My bully backed down sharpish and it was a very good feeling. Interestingly, I actually became friends with him following that fight, as his opinion of me changed. Normally, he never backed down but he did that night in front of all those people. He respected me from then on and I suppose I felt that we had finally settled things between us.

The fight with that bouncer taught me that I was no longer afraid; I liked a fight and I was good at it. That feeling of exhilaration stayed with me and it spurred me on to fight again. It was addictive.

HOOLIGAN

My brother, Brant, used to come out with me to pubs at the weekend. He wasn't really a fighter but he did get into scraps. I was still only sixteen but at that time I almost became his bodyguard, which was good practice for my future career.

I started watching Burnley FC, even though I'd been a Manchester City fan till that point. I would go to the matches at Turf Moor with my mates and my brother but we weren't there just to watch the football. In the late seventies, if you wanted a scrap then the best place to have one was at a football match. There was always someone from a rival club's "firm" who would be happy to take you on. We knew who to look for and where to find them. You could walk all the way around the ground inside the stadium back in those days, so it was easy to start something just by strolling into the rival fans' end.

I don't remember us making a big deal out of it. We weren't an organized football hooligan firm like West Ham's "ICF" (Inter City Firm) but someone did come up with the name the K-Squad, probably because there was a huge fat guy who was one of the ringleaders and he got the nickname "Kaiser." Everyone would chuck in a couple of quid each week in case someone was arrested and needed bail money and some of the fights were arranged in advance but that was about as far as the pre-planning went. It was easy enough to start something because you knew the opposition would be there.

I am not proud of it now but at the time it was the only outlet I had for all of my aggression. I didn't realize there were alternatives. We fought other like-minded individuals in groups from different football clubs, never attacked innocent bystanders and we went home and away. Somebody would hire a van to get us to other grounds and someone else had an old ambulance, which was an ironic choice of vehicle to go looking for a scrap in.

It was stupid and I was heading for trouble, but luckily for me, there was a karate instructor called Paul Armitage who lived not far from us. When he heard what I was up to he came to see my dad and told him, "You'd better get your lads to come down and see me before they end up in prison."

Encouraged by my dad, I decided to satisfy my curiosity and take a look. I went to Paul's club in an old, cold church hall to give karate a try and instantly loved it. Pretty quickly, I found that I was a natural. Because I was one of the tougher ones at the club, it didn't matter that I was a novice.

There are some places where you can learn martial arts without much physical contact, at least to begin with, but the place where I learned my karate was a fighting club. Paul was only a small bloke but he taught me a lesson early on when he kicked me hard, right in the throat. I thought I was going to die. He told me later that was to set the ground rules. That attitude stood me in good stead later in life when I used it to maximum effect in Somalia—it may have even saved my life.

There were five teams of five who fought regularly, and I was on the A team. It was unusual because there were four black belts on that team and me with my white belt. I might not have had the belts at that point but I had the timing—I could hit people and I won fights.

Inspired by my good start, I started to train hard. I also had a secret that I kept from everyone at the club. I couldn't have told anyone about it or I would never have heard the end of it. The secrecy was worth it, though, because it definitely gave me a competitive edge over my less agile opponents. I wasn't doping and it didn't involve any banned substances. Nobody had even heard of that back then. The truth probably sounds even more unlikely and I'm revealing it now for the first time after all these years, so here I go . . .

I used to do ballet.

Yes, I went to ballet classes. You can picture the scene, a strapping eighteen-year-old lad, a former football hooligan who fights big men in karate tournaments every week, creeping off to do ballet classes with a bunch of girls. Can you imagine the crap I would have taken if the others had found out about it or, worse still, actually seen me while I was dancing? I have to admit, though, I was pretty good and quite enjoyed ballet. You had to train and be disciplined about it, just like martial arts. I could even do those moves where you jump up and wiggle both feet while you are in the air. Anyway, ballet's loss was karate's gain.

Martial arts did me a huge favor because it pretty much took over my life and got me out of the football hooliganism. I quickly bought into the idea of trying to get into the national team and knew that if I got arrested I would lose my license to compete, so almost overnight I was done with fighting at football matches and I never went back to scrapping on the terraces. From when I was about seventeen onwards, martial arts played a huge part in my life and I am so glad it did. I still needed to fight but this was a way of doing it without getting into big trouble, plus I absolutely loved it and the way it made me feel. I now found I could get the same feelings of exhilaration from fighting in the kumite—the karate that involves fighting an opponent and not just learning the skills—that I used to get from fighting in the street.

It is not easy to explain the appeal of fighting to most people, who generally want to avoid it. For me, it comes from knowing you have the power over another person who is trying to beat you. That's payback for all of the hours of pain you put into training for the fight, knowing you have prepared yourself to the best of your ability, and even if you haven't, on some occasions realizing that mentally you are a strong enough fighter to still beat them. It might not look pretty but you have that to fall back on when you need it. Someone trying to hit you hard is a big thrill. It's frightening but addictive and you get a buzz from knowing you have no one to help you. It's you or them. Sometimes you can see the fear in their eyes and sometimes you can't but you end up beating them anyway.

I was glad of my martial arts skills when I came close to death as a teenager. If my reactions had not been so well honed by training I might have responded a split second too late when my car skidded suddenly on an icy road outside Burnley and that would have been the end of me. I was nineteen years old and driving over the hills to training. I'd not been driving long because I'd always ridden motorbikes when I was younger. I was going round a corner on a hill with a steep slope in an Austin Allegro. The bend was cut into the hill, which overlooked the moors before the road dropped down into Burnley. It was snowing as well and the car suddenly skidded on the ice and began to slide.

If I let it slide to my right, I would have gone over the edge and died for sure because there was a big drop. I started fighting with this out-of-control car, trying to crash it into the hill instead. One wheel slid into the mud. There was a small barbed-wire fence there and my car hit the first pole, then it went through every other pole with a thump, so I heard a boom, boom, boom as it cleaned out each one in turn without stopping. The barbed wire was going over the car and there were sparks coming from it, as it scraped against the metal.

I finally hit a large stone pillar and came to a very sudden stop. There was a massive bang as the center of the car collided with it heavily. Finally, there was silence. Somehow, I had survived, so I hobbled out of the car. My only injury was a cut to my left knee and there was blood going down my leg. I grabbed a few things and flagged down the first passing car I saw. It turned out the driver was a guy I used to know from school and he agreed to take me home.

I was in shock when I got back but I don't think I realized it at the time. I was living with my girlfriend, Melanie, and I told her I was fine. I went next door to get my neighbor, who had a truck that he could use to collect my car. I explained what had happened and he said he would go and get it.

"Do you want it back?" he asked me.

"I think it's a bit of a mess," I said, "so it might not be worth salvaging."

But he said he would bring it back anyway and I could make a decision, either way. I think he was a little surprised when he saw the car because he towed it back and brought me outside to take a look at the mangled remains.

"Were you in that fucking car?" he asked me in disbelief. It was hard to imagine that I could have been.

When the car had collided with the stone pillar, it caused a dent in the bonnet that went all the way up till it was two inches from the windscreen, which had shattered. The engine block was halfway into the passenger seat and the gear stick was through the roof where it had completely crumpled. The car was, of course, an absolute write-off and there was no part of it that he could reuse. It was almost a miracle that I survived let alone walked, or hobbled, away.

The next day, I had a massive bruise across my chest from the seat belt and it felt like my shoulders had been squashed together until they had met somewhere in the middle of my chest. I had to have a couple of weeks off work to recover.

In those days, hardly anyone ever wore a seat belt but, luckily, I did because I was uncertain in a car, though weirdly I felt safe on a motorbike because I was more used to them. I learned the value of a seat belt that day and always wore one from then on.

RED CAP

I focused on martial arts for the next few years and fought a lot of big names. Then, in 1982, Melanie got pregnant and we moved into her mum's house together. Her mum moved out to live with her boyfriend, so we had the place to ourselves until the baby arrived.

The day that Melanie's water broke also happened to be the same day I was meant to be going for my first trials with the British karate team. I was halfway out the door with my bag in my hand when it happened and I realized that I would have to stay. Thankfully, Melanie went on to have a baby girl without any complications and I became a dad for the first time at the tender age of twenty. Being our firstborn, Chamane changed everything for us and it was a new and very interesting time, with all sorts of things going through my mind. I had not long since left home and we were both still so young but fatherhood got me focusing on how I could do better for myself while thinking about the future. It was the first time I really had the idea of being self-employed one day, though that was some way off at this stage.

I had a friend who had moved to South Africa and he had said it was a great place, with good employment opportunities for a young man. That sounded good to me. Melanie and I decided to get married before I left. We had no money and I didn't even own a suit to wear on the big day. I mentioned that to a mate in the pub and he said, "Our Kenton's got a suit," and he arranged for this guy, Kenton, who I had been to school with, to lend his suit to me so I could get married in it. I stood in the registry office, wearing another man's suit, and married Melanie, then we went to her mum's boyfriend's dad's house for sandwiches and on to Melanie's brother's pub for drinks. I was a married man, as well as a father, and very aware of my new responsibilities. I already had one eye on the future.

I bought a plane ticket and blagged my way out to South Africa on a tourist visa. I stayed with my mate until I got a job working with heavy-plated metal-making machines for the mining industry, then I had to try and get the right visa to stay out there. This big South African official asked me a bunch of questions about what I had been doing in his country and he soon sussed that I had been working there illegally on my holiday visa.

"You are not supposed to be doing this, are you?" he told me sternly.

"No," I admitted, "and I am so sorry." I went on to explain why I had done it, that I had a wife and daughter to support.

I half expected him to chuck me out of the country but he heard me out then stamped my visa with a "well done, you." And that was that.

Now I had a job and it was legal, so I was able to fly Melanie and Chamane over. Meeting them from the plane was the best thing and it was so good to see my daughter again. She was growing fast.

I wanted to carry on with the karate so I went to a club and watched classes there while I waited to speak to the instructor. Obviously, he knew nothing about me and had never seen me fight but he didn't welcome my interest. Instead, he just ripped me and told me how crap everyone in England was at martial arts. There didn't seem to be any point trying to win him over, so I switched martial arts and started to do taekwondo instead. I got so good that I ended up on the national team, but South Africa still had the racist apartheid system in place at the time, so the rest of the world wouldn't engage in sport with the country, which meant they couldn't take anyone else on. I spent fifteen months out there but Melanie didn't settle in South Africa. She wasn't working and was desperately unhappy over there so when she got pregnant again we decided to leave.

Back in the UK, we moved in with my friends Stephen and Karen Burridge. Being able to stay with them was one of the nicest things that could have happened to us at the time and it was incredibly kind of them. Melanie gave birth to our daughter Janine in 1985. She was born prematurely and was very poorly in the ICU ward for weeks. At one point, she was even given the last rites by a priest. It was a terrible time and I can remember driving to the hospital worrying that she might not be alive when I got there. Thankfully, she not only survived but is absolutely fine now, with no lasting health issues.

We had Chamane, as well as baby Janine, so it was quite a full house. I started working with my dad in a cotton factory. He was a lorry driver for the company and he got me a job because I needed any kind of work just to get some money in. But I wanted something better than that. I bumped into a friend from school who was now in the military police. He told me all about it and it sounded like a nice idea. He said it was a good job and the free housing was an obvious attraction for a married man. Before I had left for South Africa, I had applied to the police force and went through all of the interviews but it was quite a long process and by the time they accepted me I was off to South Africa and it was too late. When I returned, I wrote to them again and my application was back on but the Army were quicker and they made it very clear how much they wanted me from the off, so now I had a choice to make. I picked the military because by now I was determined to become a Royal Military policeman, more commonly known as a Red Cap.

I had to go to Sutton Coldfield just outside Birmingham for three days of tests and an interview. After that, the Army told you what jobs you could do. The major who spoke to me told me I could not become a Red Cap. He wanted me to go in as an engineer because I'd been trained as one and was already skilled. He tried to tell me that it would be shit being a Red Cap, but I was adamant. I had to fight to get into the military police but in the end he relented and they let me try out for it.

In June 1985, I went down to Chichester to the Roussillon Barracks to start my training. You did the Army's basic training for twelve weeks first then three months extra training to try to become a Red Cap. I was twenty-three when I joined up and a bit older than most of the other recruits at the time, which helped. I was still a young man but one of the oldest there.

Military life is always a bit of a shock to the system but I'd done a lot of research, so I knew what I was letting myself in for. Before I joined, I spent weeks getting up at 6:00 a.m. every morning and doing a five-mile run before most people's days had even started, which helped my discipline and fitness.

Most of my mates did not think I would do well in the military because they didn't know about my martial arts training and the discipline required to do karate. I would need that if I was going to make it through. I had my hair cut short already and I was wearing the appropriate clothing when I arrived on day one. I walked into the guardroom as a civilian and a huge sergeant was standing there, looking down at me like I was a piece of shit.

"Name?" he barked.

"Lee," I said but this was not the answer he wanted.

"You can forget that fucking name in here, son! What's your second name?"

"Sansum."

He was intimidating but the most difficult thing for me was resisting the urge to grab him, pull him over the counter and knock the crap out of him for treating me like dirt. It was a feeling I would have to get used to. We were the absolute lowest of the low for weeks but I was never intimidated by any of the instructors because I knew, and they knew, that I could punch their lights out if necessary.

One of the PTIs (physical training instructors) taught unarmed combat in the gym and he was a nasty piece of work. He saw me training with the other lads and watched me fight this guy and it must have shocked him. He got everyone to try and take a truncheon away from him and he was whacking people really hard with it. How he didn't break any hands or arms I will never know. He looked over at me then and gave me a nervous look that translated as "don't take this off me" because he knew I could if I wanted to. He never gave me any shit after that.

I look back on my time there now and I can clearly recall not being scared of anybody. Ever since I beat up that bouncer at the age of sixteen, I have never been intimidated by anyone. I then gained the discipline of martial arts, which meant that it never went to my head. In the Army, I also learned to react to intimidation by controlling the very strong urge to punch someone in the face. The stakes were too high for that. I knew I couldn't mess this up. I had nowhere to live; we had two little girls and I was under a lot of pressure to pass this course, get into the Army and be deployed somewhere so we would have married quarters to live in. Meanwhile, Melanie was living with her mother in Blackpool, which was sensible because I wasn't allowed out of the base for the first two months.

Basic involved training in first aid, field and infantry skills and using weapons, as well as the all-important nuclear and biological warfare stuff, because the Cold War was still raging in the mid-eighties.

I was hoping that with all of my karate training I would find physical training in the Army pretty easy but it was extremely challenging. At first, I couldn't work out why it was so hard and I could not understand why they were throwing more and more PT at us, even when people were getting injured. It took me a long while to realize that the Army wasn't interested in training us like athletes for competition. What they were trying to do was break us.

Daft as it sounds in the modern era, the training back then was designed to wreck your body. The selection process weeds out those who are not tough enough mentally and physically. They thought that if your body breaks down it is because you are weak. For example, if someone breaks something during training they might have brittle bones and the Army wouldn't want to take them in case they broke an ankle while tabbing into battle. As people dropped off and left the course, it was usually either because they gave in or their bodies just couldn't hack it.

I struggled with this approach, even though I had trained at the national karate standard level when I was working to get into the British team. My training then was designed for me to reach peak performance, but in the military it was a test to see if you had it in you to keep going, even when you felt broken.

The instructors were horrible but I realized later that it was mostly an act. I met some of them afterwards and they were good blokes. While they were testing us, they were putting us under immense pressure, screaming and shouting so close to you that they were virtually spitting in your face, but you had to just take it. They would give us inspections all the time and you had to get everything ready in two hours, even if you had just been on the assault course and everything was covered in mud. Then you were fighting with everyone else to get stuff washed and presentable in time, which was impossible but all part of the constant pressure they applied to see if you would give in or persevere.

Once I'd passed basic, I went into phase two training to become a Red Cap. For the first month, training intensified and we were losing blokes left, right and center. We covered military law, so there was a lot of reading, basic SOCO (scene of crime officer) skills and interviewing techniques, as well as how to arrest someone and restrain them, which was straightforward for me as I was used to being taught martial arts moves. There was one thing I struggled with, though, and it really, really got to me, because it should have been simple but I found it incredibly hard. The running.

No matter how hard I tried, and despite all of my early morning runs, I was always in the last 20 percent on a run. We ran every day and it didn't matter if we were running for a mile or ten, I was always at the back of the group and it was doing my head in. How could I be gym fit but I couldn't bloody run? I tried my best and, when we had rare days off, I ran on my own to try to improve but I just couldn't get my speed up. I started to realize it wasn't my attitude. Running was just not an attribute I had within me. We saw our training sergeant and our officer quite regularly for feedback and it was always the running that they had negative comments about. Thankfully, it was the only thing I wasn't good at and I made up for it with the milling.

Milling is something that the Paras famously do but we did it as well. It looks a bit like boxing except you are not allowed to duck or dodge a blow. Instead, you have to get stuck into your opponent and try to knock the hell out of him while he is trying to do the same to you. It lasts for one very intense minute and the idea is to dominate your opponent with repeated blows to the head. Unsurprisingly, I was good at it and absolutely smashed my poor opponent. I saw him in town later; he had a badly swollen nose and two black eyes. At the end of the bout our PTI looked at me and said, "Good lad."

My reputation for being a bit useful at karate soon got round and a couple of blokes decided to challenge me. One was nick-named "Vulture" because he had a big nose and the other was Kevin, who I used to call "He-Man" because he was an abso-lutely huge bloke with a chiseled jaw. They took me on separately in the gym and I bashed them both up. When my captain saw the size of the black eye I had given Vulture he gave me a bollocking but at the end of it I knew I was okay because he smiled at me.

Years later, when I was serving in Northern Ireland, I met He-Man again while I was training with 177 Close Protection Platoon. This was the elite squad that guarded generals and other VIPs and they were the cream of the crop. The Royal Military Police took over the military's close protection work from the SAS who used to do it, so that's a sign of how good they are, and they deploy all over the world as bodyguards. This lot were all trained at the world-renowned RMP Close Protection Wing, now known as CPU (Close Protection Unit), in Longmoor, Hampshire. However, I had a bit of a bee in my bonnet about them at the time because I didn't think they were quite as good as they thought they were and I took great delight in beating them in training. I could shoot better on the range, was fitter than most of them and their OC (officer commanding) got really pissed off. He would say to them, "Why is this guy better than you lot?"

Then one day, He-Man turned up because he also got posted there. He was now even bigger. In fact, he was massive and almost immediately he challenged me to a martial arts fight in the gym. When I asked him why, he said, "Lee, I always remember that fight at the depot when you beat me. I've been doing loads of training since that day and I reckon I can take you."

I had been training since then, too, of course, and I realized that, if the two of us started going at each other, it was likely to become a war, with both of us taking a lot of punishment, but I wasn't going to back down.

"Right, okay, Kevin, I don't want to do it," I said, "but if we have to, then let's do it at 6:00 a.m. in the gym with no one there." It was important that I didn't let him have an audience.

We agreed to have this fight and Kevin came in at the allotted time when there was no one in the gym. He was wired for it and I was thinking that he was a bloody big unit, so this was going to be tough. I said, "Let's warm up first," and I offered to hold the strike shield for him while he gave it a few practice kicks. Then it was his turn to hold it and I started kicking it proper hard. I could see that, as I was kicking the crap out of this strike shield, his face was starting to turn a little bit white and that's what I wanted. I gave the shield a few more full-power kicks and then I asked him, "Are you ready to go?"

"No. I don't want to fight you, Lee," he said. Then he asked me, "How do you get so much power in your kicks? I have never felt anything like it."

This had been my plan all along. I knew when he felt the power and the speed of the kicks, he would shit himself and back down. I was bloody glad he did because I think we would have done each other some serious damage otherwise. When I am in a fight, I don't have an off switch, so you would have to knock me out to stop me and this one would have been brutal.

A long time afterwards, He-Man told me that he hadn't really wanted to fight me at all. Apparently, the OC had told him to arrange a fight with me and beat me up, to put me in my place!

The course we had to get through to become Royal Military policemen was a physically and mentally demanding one. There was always a very high failure rate and, out of fifty-four of us at the start, there were only a dozen guys left who successfully completed the course and passed out, which shows just how tough it was. We hated the instructors for always being in our faces, though we respected them, too, because we realized they knew what they were doing. There was one guy in particular, Karl, who was tall and smart and had a huge presence, which inspired me to be more like him, and I think I did a good job of it in the end. I have thanked him since we left the Army for being the example that I needed back then.

I got through the basic Red Cap course okay but I really didn't like it until it was close to the end. I thought that some of the instructors weren't very intelligent and they were asking us to do things I didn't agree with. I was a bit angry because I could see that if they just changed the training a bit, more people would get through. Looking back, I was thinking about it too much. When we reached the last stage with all of the investigation techniques, the instructors eased up on us a lot and almost became like friends because they knew by then that we were the ones who were going to pass and they would be working with us some day. Because their attitudes totally changed, I started to thoroughly enjoy it.

I have been close to dying on a number of occasions and some people joke that I have nine lives but I used up one of mine on that course, though it wasn't my fault. A guy close to me had an ND (negligent discharge) of his weapon and it could have taken my head off. There were four of us in a shelter and he had a pistol in his hand. He was sitting opposite me when somehow it went off. The bullet passed between me and another guy sitting next to me, narrowly missing us both. It must have been about three feet from my head and so close to him that it burst his eardrum and he had to leave the course because of injury.

Of course, the guy who accidentally fired it was binned, too, but not before our furious instructor had pinned him to the wall and punched him. It was not a nice sight. The guy was crying and I think he was in shock, but the fury of our instructor was understandable. I have seen the effects of a negligent discharge up close since then and it is gruesome. When you are hit by a bullet, it is not like it looks in the movies. Hollywood films still tend to show neat holes and avoid being too realistic with the gore in case it puts audiences off.

I saw the body of a soldier who was accidentally shot with a round from an SA80. It happened because weapons are usually at stage one or stage two. Stage one means your weapon is cocked and ready to fire if you flip off the safety. Stage two means your mag is on the weapon but there is no round in the breech, so it is not cocked and ready to fire. A soldier who thought his rifle was at stage two actually had his weapon at stage one and it went off accidentally, killing his mate right in front of him. This is why there are set military drills for unloading weapons because if you don't do it right, fatal accidents can happen.

You cannot mess around with weapons at any time. When I was stationed in Germany, a squaddie accidentally shot his mate in the chest with a practice round from a Milan. That's a heavy-duty guided anti-tank missile. He was fucking about with it in the armory right next to our police station and someone died as a result.

TAKING THE SHOT

My first posting was to Sennelager, near Paderborn in West Germany as part of an operational unit, which meant we went out into the field with troops. The role in combat would involve interrogating and processing prisoners of war, checking routes and signing them. At Sennelager, we had a big, real-time policing role at one of the largest military bases in the country. Virtually every soldier in NATO went there at some point, so that meant there was fighting every Friday and Saturday night once they had been out drinking, and in our role you had to get stuck in and break it all up. It was an exciting time; we were young, fit men, policing young, fit men and I was never frightened of a scrap.

It was during this posting that I finally taught myself how to run. I did that by using affirmation. It's a technique I learned from speaking to a really good runner who gave me an old, well-worn book, which promised the world's riches using a simple technique. I applied it to running, as he suggested, and this chap and that small, torn book changed my life, though I am embarrassed to admit that, after all these years, I can't remember its title. I had always done my own affirmations and had dreams and was constantly thinking about how to attain them but now I had a framework for it all. I eventually realized that I was poor at running because I was expecting failure, so I changed my way of thinking and every day and night I went through my affirmations, telling myself: "You are the best runner in the company." And, sure enough, within three months, I went from being the worst runner in the world, in my eyes, to the fastest in my company.

I have always used the technique when I really want something. Usually, if I focus on it, I generally get what I want in the end and it's something I've taught my kids to do too. Damon is a Team GB Olympic player and martial arts world champion and my daughter Janine is an inspiration to other young women as both a single mother and one of the best salespeople in her area.

I essentially tricked my brain into thinking I was a great runner and it worked. When you can fully visualize having something or achieving something like that with absolute certainty, your brain can't tell if it's real or not. I have trained loads of martial arts world champions and I always give them an example like this one: "If I got hold of Gary Lineker's brain and transplanted it into you, you would play like him and become a successful footballer. It's the brain that does that to you, not your body, so if you can change the way you are thinking then you can achieve almost anything."

As a result of the affirmation technique, I went from zero to hero at the unit. Now I was the best runner and I was the best shot too. While I was training with 177 Platoon, everyone watched as I took a Browning pistol with an extended magazine fitted and aimed it at a man-sized target ten meters away. We had put up a one-inch square of tape, the kind you use to plug bullet holes on targets, and I placed every round on that tiny square, one after the other. I visualized what I was going to do and used affirmation techniques beforehand. Every bullet found the right spot: all thirteen within the white square. It was a case of aim, shoot, pause, breathe; aim, shoot, pause, breathe and the result was the same each time.

I really enjoyed life in Sennelager. While I was there, I got to know two guys on the dog section. They were always called out on interesting stuff, like tracking wanted people or important searches, and it was seen as a prestigious job. When I heard they were both leaving, I put in for the role but loads of other people applied for it, too, and I wasn't sure if I would get the chance. In the end, I was put forward for it, which was an early indication of how I was viewed by those above me, even in my first posting. They knew I could be trusted to work well on my own.

In late 1986, I joined the police dog section after a lengthy training course with the Army Veterinary Corps. From now on, I would have a partner for my police work. He didn't say much but he was very loyal and I could always depend upon him. My dog was called Berry and I got him as a puppy. Berry was a German shepherd and I spent most of my days out walking with him and training him to become a police dog. He was a great dog and I got really attached to him.

Berry soon joined me when we were out in the town breaking up trouble. With so many squaddies in Sennelager you were guaranteed fighting every weekend and some of it got out of control. We would get a call and turn up to break up fights that were escalating. The guys who were already there, trying to deal with the scrapping, almost breathed a sigh of relief when we showed up. I often heard them say, "Yes, they are here!" when I walked in with Berry. I had my karate skills and Berry could take a man down with a "right arm true," where a police dog jumps up and latches onto a man's arm with his teeth before dragging him to the ground. If we showed up with my mate Paul and his dog, the fight would be over pretty quickly because Paul was massive and in good shape. He was six foot six and could pick up two average-sized squaddies, one in each hand, and drag them both away at the same time. He could also easily drink a crate of twenty-four beers in an afternoon while watching football.

The dogs we worked with were incredible. Given the right training, they could track people and search buildings for drugs or other stuff. I trained mine to search for arms, ammunition and Semtex, the plastic explosive that was regularly used by the IRA. I asked permission to take Berry with me when I eventually left Germany. With those skills he would have come in very handy in Northern Ireland but they wouldn't let me, so we had to part company. When I left, he really missed me and I heard that he did not respond to the next person who took him on. They couldn't train or control him. He had to be used as a "war dog," patrolling the perimeter of bases, but even that didn't work. In the end, he became too aggressive, tried to attack people and eventually had to be put down, which was very sad.

We have a dog now who wouldn't be much use in the Army because he is a bit of a coward. He's a little blue Staffy called Rogan, named after rogan josh curry, and he is even frightened of our chickens. I don't think he would be very good in a scrap.

In 1987, while we were still out in Germany, our third child, Damon, was born in Paderborn, completing our family. Unfortunately, I missed the birth because I was away on a course but was delighted that we now had a boy. I absolutely love my girls but to have two great daughters then a son seemed perfect and I was absolutely made up.

In Germany, we were given duty weapons. You didn't have personal ones, you just got whatever the last shift had handed over in the back of the duty room. It was a terrible system because you could not trust that pistol in your holster. If you needed to use it, you didn't know if the sights were a little off or if it had been damaged by a previous user. These pistols were dropped or bashed up during nighttime brawls, so you never had full confidence in them. The attitude in Germany at the time seemed to be that it didn't matter because you were never going to need it anyway, which was crazy. They might as well have given us guns without ammo.

Trust in your weapon matters and it mattered big-style on the day I was called to tackle a soldier who had suddenly gone berserk and was holding a kid at knifepoint. When we turned up, we were confronted with this squaddie with a knife pressed to the neck of a boy who could only have been about three years old. For whatever reason, he had lost it completely and was now threatening to kill his own son. We learned that he also had a daughter but she was nowhere to be seen so we were worried for her safety too. Obviously, we wanted to talk this guy into releasing the kid and giving up.

"What's going on?" I asked him. "Where is your daughter?"

"I've killed her," he told me. "She is in the flat and I am going to kill this one as well."

I drew my weapon then. He had just told us he had already murdered one of his children and given us every reason to believe he was about to kill his son as well, right in front of us. The knife was pressed hard against the little boy's neck and he was already bleeding, so I decided I was going to have to shoot this guy. I would have had no problem with putting him down if it meant saving the child. Trouble was, I did not trust the weapon I was pointing at him because it wasn't mine. I was ready and willing to take the shot but, if the sights were off, I would fire it without knowing where that round was going to land. It might miss the target and go over the bloke's head, giving him enough time to cut his son's throat. If I aimed too low with a dodgy sight then I could end up shooting the boy instead.

So, what could I do?

I decided not to take the shot, all the while hoping and praying that we could talk this crazed bloke out of killing his son right there in front of us.

He was ranting but ended up going back into his flat, which incidentally he had already set on fire. I followed him and was there when he came back out again with his son. My mate managed to grab the kid and get him out of there. We were now able to keep the bloke from doing immediate harm to anyone else and we even managed to put out the fire. We kept talking to him all the time and, in the end, he broke down and gave himself up.

His wife was in the flat too. She had been cut but thankfully was not seriously injured. Even better, he had been lying to us. He had not killed his daughter after all. She was there, too, unharmed, and that was a huge relief. Not firing my gun turned out to be the best option but I only knew that for sure with hindsight and things could have gone very differently.

In Northern Ireland, everything was different. All the weapons were personal to you because it was a war zone. They knew you might really need your gun out there one day. That's where I was posted next, but before that my military career almost ended completely.

THE BULLSHIT BLAME GAME

While I was with 110 Provost Company in Germany, I got seriously injured. I used to do a lot of sports back then, including cross-country, football, rugby, karate and basketball. One day, I went up for a basket and when I landed my legs wouldn't work anymore.

I had been overtraining and my back went. They sent me to the Army hospital and into intensive care. I was stuck there in traction for three months and due to have surgery for spinal fusion. On the day of my op, the surgeon came round and it wasn't the guy originally scheduled to do my surgery. This was a Navy doctor called Surgeon Captain Clarke. He asked me, "How old are you soldier?" and when I told him, he said, "I'm not going to cut you. It will ruin your life."

He gave me six months' sick leave instead but he also medically downgraded me, which meant I was done for and I fell into an intense depression. I had been about to try and join DET (the Special Reconnaissance Unit, also known as 14 Field Security and Intelligence Company). They were an elite unit that was trained by the SAS and very hard to join. One of their courses had a thousand applicants but only seventeen personnel passed through and were eventually deployed to Northern Ireland. I had been training hard for it with a Para friend at the unit, but the surgeon put a stop to that. He told me, "You can't do anything now. You will be lucky if you can walk properly again, lad."

I went cold turkey from the morphine, the sleeping tablets and a cocktail of other drugs that I'd been given in the hospital to deal with the pain in my back and was sent home with some simple painkillers. I guess that was the Army way, back then.

I was posted back to Catterick, in North Yorkshire, to do my rehab but I couldn't walk, stand or sit for more than five minutes and I lost a lot of weight. I had to lean against the wall to walk around the outside of the detached married quarter I lived in and was happy if I could make it round there at all. This was my process of attempting to become mobile again. I figured if I could reach the point where I could walk unaided around the quarter, I would eventually be able to run, so I started with this simple affirmation. My neighbor's kids would watch me with tears streaming down my face because of the pain.

I was in a bad way so, in desperation, I went to see an osteopath in nearby Darlington. He was a skinny guy with a beard, wearing a chunky jumper. He said he had never seen anyone with more developed back muscles because I had been doing my rehab like a loony, as I was so determined to get medically upgraded and back to normal duty. He looked at me like I was some kind of medical freak.

I was feeling very fragile by this point and all of my self-confidence had gone. I told him I would be happy if I could just run again or even walk half a mile. He got me on the bed and cracked me and I nearly shit myself at the sound but, as soon as he was done, I realized it had worked. It was a bloody miracle and, all of a sudden, I felt like I was walking on air.

I found out the details of the medical test I had to pass in order to upgrade myself and all of the questions they would ask me. I dosed myself up on ibuprofen and co-codamol and trained like a crazy man to pass the test, even rehearsing all the answers daily in my affirmations so I wouldn't weaken and put any doubt in the examining doctors' minds. I needed those doctors to sign me off as fit and ready for active duty, which they did in the end but I don't think they could believe what they were seeing because my recovery had been so dramatic.

I was medically upgraded because I managed to cheat the test but I knew I would not be able to get into any kind of specialist unit until I was fully fit again and that could be a year or two away. What could I do in the meantime that was specialized?

I liked the sound of the SIB (Specialist Investigation Branch), who were an elite unit with a role a bit like Internal Affairs or the CID (Criminal Investigation Department). They wanted brains and not just brawn, so my fitness was not such a crucial issue, but they were still incredibly difficult to get into and you had to be a cut above the rest. I had always been given the best possible reports from my superiors, so I had confidence in myself and thought that I would be up to the challenge.

First, I had to go on attachment with them for months, while they assessed whether I was good enough to even attempt to join them permanently. Then I had to take the initial Investigators course and the Advanced Investigators course as well as the SIB training course. None of that was easy and the dropout rate for SIB is insane. During selection, we were based in Chichester and it was as if we had stepped out of the military police. We had our own block inside the wire while doing our training and no one else would talk to us because of the role we were taking on. Even the officers and non-coms gave us a wide berth. It was a weird feeling.

I managed to get through all of that training, though it was the hardest thing I have ever done. The pressure was intense, with loads of testing all the way through it. Even at the very end, when I had passed all of the tests, each of us had to go and see the colonel in charge of the SIB. He grilled me like it was an interrogation. Basically, if he liked you, you were in and if he didn't, you were out. Loads of people failed at this final stage.

In 1988, I passed and finally joined the SIB, which is a very big deal in the forces. To be accepted into an elite outfit like that shows you are exceptional and it gives your confidence a massive boost. It certainly helped me later in life when I had to demonstrate that I was good enough to work as close protection for VIPs and royalty. Coming from SIB does that on its own. I was still only twenty-six years old, one of the youngest to join, and they promoted me to sergeant. I had been taking my sergeant courses and still had one left to complete at this stage but I got the rank automatically when I joined SIB.

Now, though, no one I knew in the military police would talk to me anymore. They either hated me or were too scared to speak to me, because the SIB had a fearsome reputation with the uniformed branch. Everyone was frightened of the SIB because we had almost unlimited power and they knew we used informants, so if something crooked was going on, there was a very strong chance we would get to hear about it.

I was posted to Tidworth Camp in Wiltshire and took on some massive cases. We did some great jobs but the one I remember most was the one that went badly wrong. It was a big drugs op and when it went pear-shaped, everyone above me denied all knowledge of it and there was massive fallout. There was pressure on me to accept full responsibility for this one. Some people said I was young enough to take the fall but I wouldn't do it. This was the SIB and a job I had dreamed of since my injury. It got so bad that I was even threatened with being beaten up. I said, "Fucking come on then. I'm not scared of you or being beaten up." I had been medically upgraded by now and most of my injury had gone; I'd been in the gym a lot and with doses of muscle relaxants and painkillers, which I took daily for the next fifteen years, I had my power back.

I told them I wanted to go back to regular uniform but they wouldn't let me. They threatened to send me back to a camp where I had done internal affairs jobs on the military police, including one on an officer who claimed money to put three kids in boarding school when he actually had no kids, so there was no way I could go back there.

I was going nowhere, it seemed, but then I had a stroke of luck. Someone I'd worked with before was involved in the postings and, breaking the chain of command, I went and explained the situation to him. He asked, "Where do you want to go?"

I told him the witness protection unit in Northern Ireland was my preferred option. It was out of the way and would get me out of a shit situation. He sorted it for me and when everyone found out where I was going all hell broke loose. "Fucking Sansum! How have you done this?" They wouldn't let me keep my acting sergeant rank when I left. That was a final fuck-you from the SIB.

I went to Northern Ireland to this small, under-the-radar unit to regroup and start my career again. I was fit, healthy and determined. I had only been in the military for three and a half years and was one of the youngest serving guys to join the SIB until I was downgraded and fucked over, but now I was back in the game.

BANDIT COUNTRY

I arrived in Northern Ireland in late 1989, when the province was still very much in the grip of "the Troubles," as the thirty years of sectarian violence between Catholics and Protestants were commonly called. This made it sound like a little spot of bother and not a long civil and religious war that was to claim at least 3,500 lives before it finally came to an end in the late nineties.

Arriving in Northern Ireland was a massive culture shock. As soon as I left the SIB it felt like they had cut me loose with no support but I have spoken to guys from other corps who said they felt exactly the same way when they arrived in the province. Because I was an RMP, I went in for two years when most regular Army lads were posted to Northern Ireland for just four months. I had married quarters in Thiepval Barracks in Lisburn, County Antrim, with my wife, Melanie, and our three young children and I was given a brief description of how to get to the base with all of the dos and don'ts. It immediately made me feel really anxious for my family. It was far more aggressive than I had imagined it to be.

Driving through all the checkpoints and fortifications in Belfast was a very oppressive experience. The place felt just like a war zone, which it was in every way, except officially. Everyone looked at you. They would notice your car because it had GB plates on it, not NI ones, and everyone was constantly checking out everybody else. It took a while for me to get used to this and the place left a really big visual and mental mark in my brain that has never left me.

Northern Ireland was incredibly dangerous, especially if you accidentally went into the wrong area, which could prove fatal. To avoid this, they gave us maps with color-coded areas on them. You could go into green and amber areas, but red ones were restricted. To make life more complicated, red areas and temporary red areas would change at a moment's notice due to operations that were being conducted in them, as they didn't want Army or covert troops in there at the same time. If you went into red areas, you would be court-martialed. If you were caught there dressed in civvies, you would be arrested then thrown in jail. There was no mucking about because this was serious stuff. There was a sickening incident in 1988, when two British Army corporals, Derek Wood and David Howes, who were dressed in civilian clothes, inadvertently drove up to the funeral procession of an IRA man. They were dragged from their car, severely beaten then shot dead, and all because they drove into the wrong place at the wrong time.

If you tried to buck the system or you didn't check the latest area status, you could stray into a temporary red zone. That might cause the kind of confusion that results in what's known as a blue-on-blue, where someone shoots someone from their own side.

When you were passing through an area, you were given a transit route and you had to stay on that route or you would be in trouble. You had to book out every time you left camp, irrespective of what you were doing, and book back in again. This wasn't just petty bureaucracy. If you didn't return, people would have to come out and look for you, putting themselves in danger in the process.

There was everything you needed on camp, including a NAAFI (Navy, Army and Air Force Institutes) to run everything and a shop. I also have to give the Strip a mention. This was a row of a dozen Portakabins all done up like bars and nightclubs, so people could go out on the lash safely without leaving the barracks. There would be guys in there from units that had been in the field for months, and busloads of Paras would come in, too, who would sometimes smash the place up. There were admin girls from the camp or sometimes local girls who were bused in to make it feel like a permanent party. The military police were banned from going into the Strip, so there were some outrageous nights with people getting absolutely shitfaced. It was wild, like something out of a Vietnam war film. One of the bars used to play "We Gotta Get Out of This Place" by the Animals on an hourly basis and followed it with all of the Vietnam-era songs. You could have imagined you were in Saigon, and the atmosphere was heightened by the place being almost in darkness. There was just a bit of red lighting, so it could not be seen and targeted from the outside by mortars fired by the Provisionals. The military police had to patrol the perimeter looking for mortar base plates. What a place.

You were allowed to go into Lisburn but it was really restricted as we were only a few miles south of Belfast. Pubs would go in and out of bounds constantly as intelligence picked up threats. The kids went to school outside the wire there because it was a Loyalist area, so it was safe for them, but there were still red areas in Lisburn that you were not allowed to go into. These were the really tough Loyalist, Orange areas. The Army patrols kept Lisburn as safe as possible, so they could operate there, with some of the families even living on estates outside the wire. The area was saturated with UDR (Ulster Defence Regiment) patrols to maintain some level of normality, and the routes in and out of Belfast always had permanent Army and RUC (Royal Ulster Constabulary) checkpoints, as well as snap checkpoints thrown up now and again.

My first role in Northern Ireland was pretty close to my later career as a bodyguard and I certainly developed skills there that stood me in good stead when I went into close protection later, including a constant state of vigilance that became second nature to me in the province. I wound up working in 173 Military Police Company. Not many wore uniforms, and everybody grew their hair longer than the uniformed guys to fit in with the locals and worked covertly. They were an amalgamation of lots of different small units, each with its own specializations, and they did loads of different stuff, including my new role in witness protection and legal affairs.

The circumstances of my stint in witness protection were pretty bizarre. The IRA had worked out that it might be a good idea to bog down the Brits in a lot of paperwork, time and expense, responding to often spurious legal claims from civilians. Subsequently, there were a large number of cases from lawyers on behalf of clients who claimed to have been assaulted or victimized by the military, at checkpoints perhaps or in their homes. These allegations all required investigation and often resulted in court cases, where serving or former members of the military were called as witnesses. In places like South Armagh or the heart of Belfast, it meant putting those men at considerable personal risk. Terrorists keen to target these witnesses for their association with the British Army would know exactly where they would be and when because the legal process made that information public.

Before the trials, we kept the witnesses safe at Moscow Camp, the naval barracks inside Belfast shipyard, but the really dangerous time was when they arrived at court and left, following their testimony. Even with a police presence, courts in areas like this could still be targeted, so we had to find ways to outwit the terrorists. Sometimes we would arrive before anyone else, pulling up outside at 6:00 a.m., and on one occasion, we hired a beat-up old van and pretended to be builders arriving to do a job there. We had to resort to these methods because the paramilitaries had "dickers" looking out for us. If these paramilitary lookouts spotted us escorting a witness, they'd know our faces for next time and our cover would be blown. We would then become targets ourselves so there was a lot resting on our ability to get these men in and out of court without being spotted.

In Northern Ireland, you had to search your car every time before you got into it. That meant getting down low, so you could look underneath and check if anyone had planted an IED there. We were issued with a device that was supposed to bleep if it sensed a bomb but it was next to useless, so we had to rely on the old "mark one eyeball" instead and have a good look at it. That was fine when you were leaving home, but if you didn't want to be seen doing it, you had to be craftier. I would open my door then hang out of the car with my head low so I could check underneath it. Sometimes, we came back to the car after we had parked it in areas where we couldn't check it in case a dicker spotted us and worked out we were undercover Army, then we would never be able to use that vehicle in the area again as it would become a target. This left us with a big problem. What if someone already suspected us and had planted a bomb in the car while we were away from it?

I would take my seat belt off as we were arriving so I could get out of the car quickly and I always kept it off when we drove away again. I would leave the door off the catch and very slightly open and hold onto it. If there was a bomb under the car, the thinking was that you would be more likely to be blown out of a vehicle that way and might survive the blast. Sometimes, if we were returning to the car in a really shit area, we would look at each other and think, *Here we fucking go.* All you could do was climb in, start the engine, put your foot down and hope.

This routine of checking your vehicle when you could and praying when you couldn't became a normal part of everyday life. Nowadays, when I am teaching vehicle search to others, there is an intensity to that training session because I have been in places where it really mattered and my life depended on it.

There were areas of Northern Ireland where driving at all was discouraged. South Armagh was known as "bandit country" and everyone traveled around it by chopper because it was considered too dangerous to go anywhere by road. At least, that was the accepted view but, for a year or more, my mate and I drove around it in our beat-up old Renault, working ops undercover. We had long hair and wore baggy civilian clothes to keep our gear hidden under them and we tried to look as little like Army as possible.

One day, we had been down to Keady in Armagh to speak to someone there. On our way back, we called into Bessbrook military base for one very important reason: I liked the food there. Bessbrook was a fort and the biggest helicopter base in Europe. I spotted a mate at the base. He had just come off a stint on one of the Army 'Golf' towers that were a very visible part of the military presence in South Armagh. Everybody lived underground below these towers, then they would go up to the top to look around as it was the safest way to observe the area. He was about to get on a helicopter to go back to Lisburn because his tour was over. He was eager to get back as quickly as possible so he could go on the piss but there was no sign of the chopper, so I said, "Why don't you come back with us?"

"How did you get here?" he asked.

I pointed to the beat-up old Renault. "In that car over there."

"Fuck off," he said. "I'm not driving back with you in that. You're going to die!"

"No, mate," I said. "It's safe. We do it all the time."

But he was having none of it. As far as he was concerned, the roads in Armagh were completely unsafe and that was that. He was going to sit tight and wait for his helicopter ride. We said goodbye, drove back to Lisburn without incident and put all our weapons away then went to the mess. My mate was there already, as his chopper had finally showed up and it could travel a lot faster than us. He was as pissed as hell and he looked in a right state. He saw us and started shaking his head.

"Mate, what happened?" I asked him.

"We went up in the helicopter and we got shot to fuck!" he told me.

It appeared that the paramilitaries had been waiting for something to aim at that day and his ride home was just what they wanted.

"There were rounds coming through the chopper!" he said. "I thought you bastards were mad for driving back and that I was safe but I should have come with you!"

He was lucky that none of those rounds hit him as they went through the helicopter, but he was right about the roads too. They could be very dangerous and I soon learned just how bad they were. We were driving back from South Armagh and a car started driving aggressively behind us. Were they Provos (Provisional Irish Republican Army) and had they worked out who we were? We didn't want to hang about to find out.

We pulled ahead, went round a corner and there, right in front of us, was a tractor, slap-bang in the middle of the road, blocking it completely. On one side of us was a steep hill and there was a cliff on the other. We had nowhere to go. We couldn't get round the tractor or ram it and that car was pulling up behind us. We were right in the middle of bandit country and this looked a lot like an ambush. We had no choice but to stop and wait to see what happened next. We cocked our weapons and started talking through what we were going to do because we fully expected someone to get out of that car and start shooting. We sat there and waited, fully expecting to die.

But that didn't happen and I have no idea why. In the end, the guy pulled his tractor over and, as we drove by, we saw some blokes on the side of the road and they were laughing at us. We didn't know who they were but it looked like they might have worked out who we were, even though we were in civilian clothes. Of course it is possible they hadn't realized we were undercover Army at all and that's why they let us through, or perhaps they just weren't planning on taking out two guys in a car that day. I'll never know.

That was a one-off and nothing like it ever happened again, but the incident had a profound effect on me. I realized that if things had gone differently, I could have easily died that day. Knowing that meant I accepted the situation and I didn't fear it. I became very confident from then on, in fact, because my judgment was never clouded by fear.

The things we were doing in Northern Ireland were extremely dangerous, but the longer you stay somewhere, the less you think about the risks. Your brain compensates for them and you accept that danger as part of your life.

ABSENTEES AND DESERTERS

After twelve months of witness protection, I wanted to move into the FRU (Force Research Unit), a covert military intelligence unit set up to penetrate terrorist organizations, as I had liaised with them on cases and gotten to know them all. They wanted me because I was ex-SIB and they reckoned they could utilize my skills, but I wasn't allowed to request a transfer to them. In the end, I joined 175 Provost Company in a broader police role. This was a proper military police field operational outfit. I took an investigation role. There were four of us working on what were termed "protracted investigations," which had been going on for some time and they were hard to do in what was effectively a war zone.

My boss let me do what I wanted, which was great, but my speciality here was the "As & Ds"—the absentees and deserters that we had on file. I'd had a lot of success bringing in deserters while I was based at Catterick and I wanted to carry on with the work. I was handed a big file full of names of people who were originally from Northern Ireland and had deserted from the military, from the Irish regiments or the Paras, and there were also regular signals communications sent to us on people who were in Northern Ireland who shouldn't have been there. I was shocked to find hundreds and hundreds of outstanding names in that file.

"What is going on with this?" I asked.

"Nothing," I was told. "Just log it."

I didn't come to Northern Ireland just to record the fact that no action had been taken against absentees and deserters and leave it at that.

"But who is going out and getting these guys?"

"No one. You can't. It's too dangerous."

Of course, the situation in Northern Ireland was always dangerous but you couldn't use that as an excuse to let off every deserter from the province. I protested because these people were obviously living out in the community, so we should try and bring them in. I made it my mission to get as many of them as possible and I started grabbing them one by one.

Signals would come into us with suspected locations of deserters and I would go after them. It was exciting work, and because I was left to my own devices, there was almost zero paperwork. I would make a plan with the RUC and local military commanders so I could go in and get these people out. I even grabbed someone from a wedding. All I did after lifting one of them was contact the office in London and the deserter's CO, informing them that the guy had been picked up.

We had a tip-off that two deserters were planning to attend this wedding and one of them was going to be the best man. We decided to get them both. The guys were soldiers who had served in West Belfast. They met a woman while out patrolling and struck up a friendship, which did happen from time to time, and now one of their mates was about to marry her. The Army would not give soldiers permission to visit the province, especially that part of the city, and these types of relationships were frowned upon. But some of the lads would go into Ulster without permission and that alone would mean they were in an OOB (out of bounds) area, which in itself was a court martial offense.

These deserters were now in a dangerous Loyalist area just off the Shankill Road that was hemmed in by IRA-controlled areas. They didn't seem to understand how dangerous that was for them. It was massively high-risk. The presence of soldiers in plain clothes was enough to spark civil unrest by itself. Everyone knew everybody in these areas and gangs of men would quickly form to go looking for touts who might be suspected of feeding information about the paramilitaries to the authorities. This might cause riots and the consequences could be fatal for idiots like these two.

The day before this wedding, we went down to the bride's house in West Belfast in numbers, with the RUC putting a massive police cordon around the location. There must have been fifty or sixty men involved in the operation to raid this one home. We burst in and went straight into the living room of this scummy house and everyone was in there drinking. We quickly established that one of the men we were looking for was present.

"You are coming with us," I told him and that prompted lots of shouting from the other guests who were determined to prevent us from taking him.

We didn't have time for an argument or for anyone to resist us. We had to get in and out again with that deserter as fast as we could before the IRA heard about us being there and mounted a response. Even though it was a Loyalist area, the Provos could get an ASU (Active Service Unit) or a sniper down there quickly, if they knew they had a target. They had done it before. It was another reason to arrest Army deserters because they were risking their lives just by being in this area so close to IRA strongholds. Any delay risked the lives of every man with us, but the guests at this pre-wedding party were on their feet, being vocal and obstructive and they would not shut up.

I pulled my Browning then and told them, "He is coming with us and if any of you fuckers try to stop us, you are getting this." At the sight of my pistol, they all sat down pretty quick. It was a bit brutal but we had to do it to get this idiot out.

That was one down but the best man was still at large and the wedding scheduled for the next day. Only one thing for it. Gatecrash. They probably weren't expecting us to do that. There would be too many people present to publicly arrest him; we'd more than likely start a riot involving all of the guests if we tried, even if we turned up mob-handed with dozens of RUC men in support. The best man must have been feeling pretty confident because he turned up, but the rest of his day didn't go quite as he had planned.

While the wedding reception was going on, one of our lads went round the back of the venue and got in behind the stage during the dance. He asked the DJ to tell the best man to come backstage because there were some presents for the couple there. The guy fell for it, and as soon as he appeared, my mate grabbed him. He bundled him out of there and away. We'd nabbed the best man before anyone else at the wedding even noticed.

This might sound a bit harsh. The guys we lifted were now facing a court martial and would probably end up doing prison time in Colchester before being kicked out of the military, but they could still consider themselves lucky because that was a lot better than dying at the hands of the IRA.

Other men weren't so lucky. I had been having a fairly quiet shift one night when the phone rang. It was a chief inspector in the RUC. He told me, "There is something happening down here in the Shankill. It's looking like we might have a riot on our hands though we don't know what it's all about yet, but there is a guy here in one of our cells and we think he might be one of yours. He isn't cooperating or telling us anything but we reckon he might know what's going on." Then he warned me, "He is a dangerous man, very aggressive, and he went a bit crazy on us. He trashed the cell and has beaten one of our guys up; can you get down here?"

Me and my mate shot down to the police station that was just off the Shankill Road and we went into this man's cell. We took one look at him and just knew that he was a squaddie.

"Stand up!" we ordered, then demanded, "Who the fuck are you?"

He got up and stood to attention but just looked at us and didn't say anything.

I walked out of the cell with the chief inspector and asked him to leave the bloke with us for a bit to see if we could get him to talk. While I was out of the cell, my mate decided not to waste any time at all. He took out his Browning and threatened to stuff the gun into this bloke's mouth. He was shouting at him, "You tell us who you are right now, or I'll blow your fucking head off!"

I thought, *Woah, that's a bit too much,* but it worked because the bloke immediately started talking.

He told us he was with a unit stationed in Berlin. Eight of them had come back to wherever it was they were from in Ireland. None of them were originally from Belfast, but unbelievably they had arranged to meet up with a mate of theirs who was from the city to go out on the piss with him. They had started drinking in people's houses, then they had gone out onto the streets in the Shankill. This was suicidal behavior because the Protestant paramilitaries had dickers out everywhere. They soon spotted these guys and assumed they were touts because they were not from the area. Everyone knew everybody else there and you could not fart without it being known about.

The paramilitaries soon caught these blokes and started beating the fuck out of them. The squaddies were hiding from the angry mob in people's houses and they were shitting themselves. We had to go out with the RUC to try and find them and save them from being literally beaten to death.

We burst through the door in this house where the family were trying to hide one of the soldiers from the paramilitaries. We found him there and he was a right mess. We got him away from the area and then found more of these lads in various locations but we had to put on a big operation to find and rescue them.

It took a while but we finally managed to round up nearly all of the missing soldiers between us until only one was left, still unaccounted for. Where the bloody hell was he? Had he been imprisoned in some house or flat? Was he being beaten and tortured? Was he already dead in a street somewhere?

Eventually someone told us he had been found lying in the road and taken to the hospital. "They fucked him up," our witness explained. "A taxi took him there."

You might have thought that would be the end of the matter, but this soldier was still far from safe. Unfortunately, the taxi had taken him to Belfast Royal Hospital instead of the military hospital because they didn't know who he was. The Belfast Royal was a known IRA hospital, as it was heavily infiltrated by their sympathizers. Word would soon reach the paramilitaries that there was a badly injured soldier recovering there.

Once that happened, an ASU would be on its way to finish him off where he lay. Ironically, the Loyalists had beaten him up so badly that it would now be a simple job for their Catholic paramilitary rivals to murder him while he lay helpless in his hospital bed.

We had to get there first if we were going to have any chance of saving him. Two of us sped down there, hoping we wouldn't arrive at exactly the same time as the IRA Active Service Unit. It is hard to explain the level of danger we were all in at this point, especially him. Even getting into a traffic accident in Belfast and being taken to the wrong hospital could be fatal. As a soldier in the British Army, once the IRA knew where you were, you wouldn't have long left to live.

Me and my mate bombed down there and burst in. We had to find out where he was in the hospital and we didn't have time to ask nicely, so we were being pretty aggressive about it in order to get the information we needed.

We found his ward and there he was on the bed, badly injured, with wires sticking in him and surrounded by doctors. He was barely conscious but able to look at us. We ignored the doctors, grabbed him, got him upright and pulled the wires out of him. Then we held onto him, took him out of the hospital, bundled him into our car and drove away. We went straight to Musgrave Park, the British Army hospital, and handed him over. We reasoned he would be safe there and, thankfully, he was.

On another night it might have been different. A couple of years later, the IRA planted twenty pounds of Semtex in a tunnel at Musgrave Park hospital. It was close to the military wing and, when the bomb went off, it killed two soldiers who were recovering there. The blast also injured a small child and a baby in the nearby children's ward.

We managed to get those soldiers out of harm's way in the end, though they all took a hell of a beating before we could get to them. It was a night of massive exhilaration and quite a lot of fear because the situation was so confused and uncertain for everyone involved. Nobody seemed to know what was going on at first but we just had to get on with it, do our jobs and sort it out. It was an evening I will never forget.

HONEYTRAP

I was in Belfast just off the Shankill Road, the Loyalist area where their paramilitaries were based. I needed to take a look at something on the other side of the street and I saw a gap in heavy traffic so I ran across the busy road. I had my Browning in a chest holster, which I didn't normally wear, and, as I was running, it dropped out!

I felt it go but I had no choice but to keep running to avoid a car that would have hit me. I ran across two lanes of traffic and when I looked back I could see my Browning High Power lying there in the fucking road. I had just dropped a loaded pistol, with thirteen rounds of ammunition and considerable stopping power, and I could not let it fall into the wrong hands. More importantly, I was now unarmed.

Losing your weapon is a serious no-no. Losing it in Northern Ireland, right next to the Shankill during the Troubles, was even worse. If I didn't get it back, I was totally screwed. I did not know what would be worse—the court martial or the piss being taken out of me forever for being the guy who lost his pistol. The traffic was whizzing by, preventing me from getting back to retrieve it, but now people had noticed the gun and I was praying no one ran off with it. They were still just standing there at this point, staring at my pistol. They didn't know where it had come from but they could all see it. I thought, *I have got to get there before one of you picks my gun up*, but I couldn't get through the traffic speeding by.

I had to go for it so I legged it over the road again, stopping the cars before they ran me over by waving my hand at the drivers. I was completely compromised but I managed to get to the Browning and bent to pick it up as discreetly as possible. I got back to our car and jumped in and we bugged out of there as quickly as we could.

It was a massive relief to get my pistol back and I felt a bit stupid but accidents like that happen and I've witnessed them everywhere I have been. It doesn't matter how professional or highly trained you are, they still happen. Of course, it was my fault because I hadn't properly secured my weapon but I got away with that one. I'm just glad I didn't inadvertently donate my gun to a terrorist.

As my efforts to round up absentees and deserters continued, I began to get better connections with the RUC and Special Branch. Then, one day, I got a call that put me in serious danger. I was sitting in the office on an evening duty when an inspector from Special Branch called to tell me about a squaddie who had done a tour in Northern Ireland then been posted to Germany. Apparently, he had left there and gone AWOL so he could come back to Ireland to see a local girl he'd met while he was doing "chat-up" on checkpoints. That's when the Army patrols speak to the people in cars after they have stopped them. You were not literally supposed to chat up the girls but that's what he had done and now he was smitten enough by this one to come back to her.

Through the intelligence network in Northern Ireland, Special Branch had heard that he was at the girl's house in South Armagh and they gave me an address there. They had also learned that this was a honeytrap and an IRA Active Service Unit was on its way to kill him.

Shit! We would have to move fast if we were going to rescue this idiot from one of the most dangerous locations in the province. The place was called bandit country for a reason: 123 soldiers and 42 RUC men were killed there by the IRA during the Troubles.

I immediately called the local infantry commander and asked him to help us get this AWOL squaddie out of there, but he told me there was no way he was going to do that. They'd had a riot the night before and people had been shot. "It's too dangerous," he told me. "We are not going out again for this little twat. He is on his own."

I was senior corporal and I managed to get my mate to go out there with me but there were still only two of us, which was nowhere near enough for an operation like this one. In desperation, we drove down to the local RUC station at Newtown Hamilton. We told the guy in charge that we needed their help to get the man out. He replied, "Fuck that, we are not going down there. We'll all be killed." Before pronouncing his verdict on our man's fate: "He's fucking had it."

I was in phone contact with that Special Branch inspector in London and I told him, "We are down here, we're ready to rock and roll but we can't get in. The military won't go, the RUC won't do it and we can't go in there on our own because there are only two of us."

The Special Branch inspector was getting intel fed back to him from an informer on the ETA of that ASU. "The IRA are getting close," he told me. "They will be there in an hour." But we couldn't do anything about it.

On the next call he told me, "They will be there in half an hour!" We were helpless. We couldn't get this squaddie out of there on our own and all we could do was wait it out. It was so bloody frustrating. I knew this bloke would be killed if we didn't go in now and get him.

At 10:00 p.m., the RUC had a shift change, which meant there was a new man in charge. I saw him come in and he was a big guy. He looked like a man's man and obviously commanded respect there. He asked us who we were and what we were doing there and I told him about the squaddie who was going to die if we didn't get to him.

"Right, men!" he said. "We are fucking going!"

Yes! We were going in!

We mounted up straight away and got into one of the four RUC armored vehicles they were using for the job, but we knew we were cutting it very fine. It was going to be a race against time and a bloody close one. We were driving down to that house as fast as we could but so was the IRA Active Service Unit. If we didn't get there before them, our squaddie was a dead man, but if we both arrived at the same time, there was going to be one hell of a shoot-out in that street.

The address was in a part of South Armagh, which was about a twenty-minute drive away. I can still remember the tension in that vehicle on the way there and vividly recall what it was like that night. It was November 1990, so the air was crisp and the fog was just settling and a frost starting. Everyone was getting psyched up for a gun battle and, as we drew nearer, people were shouting, "Here we go!"

This was going to be rough. We reached the street and jumped out of the armored vehicles. The RUC fanned out, taking cover and deploying around the house with their rifles aimed in case the IRA suddenly appeared around the corner. We ran up to the house, smashed the door down and burst in. It was dark but we had torches. Someone came round the corner straight at me and, without hesitation, I banged them out cold. When there is no time to think you have to act decisively to protect the lives of yourself and others. That's an attribute every bodyguard needs. I thought then and still believe now that he was there to meet the IRA unit and take them straight to that squaddie because no one else stirred in that house, even after we smashed the door in.

There was a lot of shouting while we went room to room, desperately searching for him. We crashed through a bedroom door and the woman was there but she was alone. The bloody bloke wasn't there! What the hell? Had they got him already or was he never there to start with? Did we all just risk our lives for nothing?

Then my mate shouted, "He's in here!"

I ran into the other room and found this little private in a sleeping bag. He had a broken leg and was on crutches. I didn't know what the story was behind that and I didn't care. We just grabbed him and dragged him out of there. He was either stark naked at this point or just wearing his boxers; I can't remember but his modesty was the least of our worries, and his. We needed to save this idiot's life and had no time to spare to allow him to put his clothes on.

We got him out, dragged him to the vehicle, threw him in and off we went! The idiot was gobbing off at us because he was actually annoyed we had lifted him. He was a daft, young Scottish lad who did not have the sense to realize the danger he was in. He didn't seem to understand the very perilous situation he had placed all of his rescuers in either. I was on the left and he was sitting in the middle between us, mouthing off. He would not shut up. I was so annoyed that he had put everyone in danger, including the twelve RUC men who bravely risked their own lives to get him out, and I decided to shut him up. Violence isn't always the answer but in a high-pressure environment where lives are at risk it is sometimes the quickest and most effective solution. I elbowed the ungrateful git in the side of the face and knocked him out cold. It was the only way to silence him.

We were in and out of there within minutes. We got the squaddie back, stuck him in a boilersuit, dropped him off at Lisburn and handed him over. They stuck the stupid bastard in jail for going AWOL but at least he was alive. Looking back on it now, it was an incredibly dangerous situation and the positive outcome was down to fortunate timing. Although it turned out well, things could have gone very differently and might have ended badly for all of us.

SNIPER

From time to time, when it was busy, during the Queen's visit to the province for example, every man would be deployed to back up "the Greens," as we called the rest of the regular soldiers, who comprised 99 percent of our unit. They went out patrolling areas and checking things in a normal infantry role. Some days, a platoon might have men down due to illness and they would ask for some of our guys to patrol with them. I would always volunteer, sometimes with unexpected consequences.

We were out on a patrol, tasked with clearing a route that the explosives truck took to the quarry in North Belfast. They used explosives there for blasting and the IRA had stolen them in the past. You had to drive the route, then we patrolled off it on foot, looking for command wires that might trigger explosives and any other suspicious activity. It was always dangerous, but this time, before we went out, the intelligence officer came into our briefing, which didn't normally happen. He told us the bad news: "We have heard there is a sniper out there and our intel is that you are going to get shot at. There is nothing we can do about that, so good luck." He was basically telling us someone was likely to die on our patrol and then he left us to process that information.

We patrolled a rural area in North Belfast that was close to the quarry for three hours, knowing there was a sniper out there somewhere, waiting for us. He was going to shoot at us and there was nothing we could do about it. When you are given orders, you have to do the job. You can't just say, "I don't fancy that. I'm not going." So, for three hours, you shit yourself. It was really bad.

The intelligence guy said we had other people out there on the ground, meaning Special Forces guys that I assumed were looking for this sniper, so that meant that we were basically the bait. It is hard to describe how that feels, knowing that at any moment you could be killed. It was a very quiet time because everyone spent a fair amount of it thinking about the possibility of dying and we all had to make peace with the idea.

Every tree or bush could have shielded this guy from view while he took aim at our patrol from a distance and brought at least one of us down, but we carried on. We looked for those command wires but found nothing and cleared the route the explosives truck was going to take. Then we waited on high ground and watched it come up the hill from the city.

In the end, we got through that patrol and nothing happened. If there really was a sniper out there that day, he didn't fire at us, for whatever reason. The relief was huge. As soon as we got back to barracks afterwards, we all went straight to the mess and got very pissed.

A month later, we were out on patrol again. Our call sign was Charlie Delta but we were more commonly known by our nickname, the "cheese dicks." It was Christmas 1990. It was pissing down and I was absolutely freezing. That day, we had all received packages that were initially sent out to the troops in the Gulf prior to the first war with Iraq. They had too many of them, so they delivered the surplus ones to us in Northern Ireland.

There was nothing going on in the Gulf at this stage because the actual fighting didn't begin until the middle of January with Operation Desert Storm. So the troops out there weren't doing much and we were as busy as ever. The public were sending them presents and vocally supporting them, which was fine, but we were still fighting in Ireland and it felt as if we had been forgotten. To be honest, some of the lads resented getting these packages that weren't even meant for us.

I decided not to open mine yet but to save it until I was really pissed off during this cold, wet and miserable night patrol that I was on. At least then it might cheer me up a little bit at a low point.

Eventually I reached the stage where I was so cold that, as soon as I was back in the vehicle, I decided now was the time to open it. Maybe there would be something worth having in there, even if it was just a chocolate bar.

I opened my parcel and found three things inside. The first item the Army had sent me was a box of Steritabs, which are handy for cleaning dirty water when you are fighting in the desert but less useful in a place that has actual tap water. The second object in my parcel was a bottle of factor-fifty sunscreen, which is useful in Kuwait but less so in Northern Ireland during the winter. The final item was even more spectacularly pointless. It was a packet of Durex condoms. It was as if the Army had actually decided to send me the three most useless items a man could possibly receive while on duty in a cold, wet, miserable and solitary Northern Ireland. I took one look at it all and thought, *Merry fucking Christmas!*

If you are forced to take on an armed paramilitary with your bare hands, you know you are in trouble. I was faced with that scenario in a massive housing estate outside Lisburn. I can't say what I was doing there that night, even now, but it was late, around midnight, and we were walking back through a really bad Protestant area. There were four of us and we were all unarmed. It was dead quiet with no one else around, until we suddenly saw this bloke standing there. It was obvious he was a dicker—a lookout for the Protestant paramilitaries who controlled the area. He was a tall guy, roughly shaven and dressed in normal clothes. Because of his stance and the way he was carrying himself, I had no doubt he had a gun. They always did. The paramilitaries wouldn't put a man on the street to stop suspicious people without one. As we drew closer, he stepped from the shadows and demanded to know, "Who the fuck are you?"

None of us said anything. We shouldn't have been there and we had no explanation that would have satisfied him. We knew he was armed and that we had to get away from him fast or we would be in deep shit. You might think that supposedly Loyalist paramilitaries would be on our side. They were pro-British and anti-Catholic, as well as sworn enemies of the IRA. It didn't work like that. Ironically, Army patrols of uniformed soldiers passing through that area would have been fine but undercover operatives walking round in plain clothes were a very different matter. They represented a clear threat to the Loyalists who were terrified of informers, or "touts," passing information about them to us.

The dicker demanded to know who we were and what we were doing there and of course we couldn't tell him. I knew that his next move would be to pull a gun and raise the alarm. Soon we would be surrounded by paranoid paramilitaries demanding to know the names of our informants. If that happened, we were in big trouble. At a bare minimum, we would be beaten and tortured. I wasn't going to let that happen. I knew I had to take out the dicker.

I was standing to his right, trying to look subservient while he challenged us. I had to go for it now before he raised the alarm. I would only get one shot at him and it had to count or we would all be dead. I would normally have gone for a blow to the head but he was at the wrong angle. I did have a clear shot at his chest, though, so I hit him right in the center of it as hard as I could; it almost felt as if I'd put my fist right through him. I immediately knew it was a good shot. His head went straight down onto his chest, and he just dropped like a stone. When you hit someone properly, they fall where they stand. He was out cold. I wasn't even sure that I could knock someone out with a blow to the chest, whether that was even possible, but apparently, I could and it was. The evidence was now lying unconscious in the street at my feet. We didn't hang about waiting for anyone else to arrive. Off we went.

BOMB

In Northern Ireland, like every soldier who had ever been sent there during the Troubles and the civilians who called it home, I had to live with the constant possibility of a bomb blast. The IRA did not engage the British Army in battle. Instead, they and the other paramilitaries used snipers and car bombs against us.

We were patrolling Lisburn city center on foot when we got the shout over our radio. The Provos had planted a car bomb and it needed sorting now. We were the closest patrol but it was on the other side of the city. The message sent all eight of us running at full speed through the city center for over a mile to get there in time.

Because of the imminent danger of a massive blast from this vehicle bomb, we couldn't risk being out in the open. For all we knew, it could go off at any time, so after clearing local residents out of houses and emptying pubs and cafes, me and a mate of mine sat down and sheltered behind a wall. I was weighed down with equipment on my back, including our ECM (electronic counter-measures), which reduced the risk of the bomb being detonated remotely by radio control. So I had a lot of gear and a bloody big gun. Next thing, we hear someone on the radio asking, "Who has checked those houses next to the vehicle with the IED in it?" And we realized that nobody had told those residents to get out.

Another radio message crackled: "Has anyone got eyes on those houses?"

Shit. I looked at my mate and I could tell that he was thinking what I was thinking. We were both due to be posted out soon and the last thing we needed right now was to risk our lives popping out from behind a nice bit of protective wall to run round in the open, warning everyone. If the bomb went off while we were doing that, they would be finding bits of us for days. Trouble was, we were the nearest and no one else was likely to do it.

"Oh, for fuck's sake," I said, and that was the signal for both of us to get up off our arses and run out from behind cover, to risk our necks banging on doors and shouting for everyone to get out now. I felt so vulnerable. We were less than twenty meters from the IED. We knew that at any moment the bloody bomb could go off and we would both be casualties you'd hear about on the evening news.

Obviously, we didn't hang around. As soon as the job was done, we ran back toward the wall to take cover behind it, but it was much quicker to go over it than run round it. No problem normally but I was weighed down with all of that heavy equipment and when I landed it was too much for my old back injury, which instantly went again. The pain was indescribable. I was in complete agony.

I knew straight away what it was and I had to dose myself up heavily on painkillers just to get through the rest of my tour. At least this time I knew what to do. Once I got home, I went to see an osteopath at the first available opportunity. I told him what it was and what needed doing and he soon cracked me back into shape again. Job done.

Oh, and if you are wondering about the bomb, they decided to take no chances with it. They put a charge in to blow it up but, even then, it didn't go off, so disposal experts went in and defused it. Turns out I'd thrown myself over that wall and got badly injured trying to avoid a premature blast from a bomb that didn't even go off when they tried to blow it up. Of course, I had no way of knowing that at the time.

The experience I gained in Northern Ireland was really useful. I look back on it as a massive training ground for me and ideal preparation for my future career as a bodyguard, but there was one key difference from regular training: the risk. When I teach someone something, if they get it wrong in training it doesn't matter, but over there, if you got it wrong you were dead.

Because I was working undercover, in civilian clothing, in such a dangerous area, my observational and awareness skills became insanely finely tuned. I worked on them and practiced and practiced until I could remember everything: places, faces, names, rooms and their contents. I could walk into a room and remember where everything was afterwards. I threw myself into my work, day in, day out, for two years, in a constant state of alertness, which really equipped me for working in close protection later.

That Northern Ireland awareness level will never leave me. When I was working for Mohamed Al-Fayed, I went round to see a guy and he wasn't in. I saw him later and he mentioned he had been out at the time and I said that I noticed his computer was still on, so I figured he hadn't been gone for long. He must have been curious about that because he asked me what else I had noticed. I said, "Your bin was out; it was wet on the floor and your wet coat was hanging up." I then described everything in his house and I hadn't even been inside it. He was shocked by what I could recall about his home just from looking in the window, but it was second nature to me. That level of awareness and recall was one of the biggest things I took away from my time in the province.

The situation in Northern Ireland was very complex, but when you were on the ground it was worth remembering something quite simple: the IRA wanted to kill you. The republicans hated us, and not just the paramilitaries; the people did too. When you went into IRA areas, as we did often, you had to be on your A-game, every time. In South Armagh, when you left an IRA-controlled area to go into a Loyalist one, it was a "phew" moment. Now we were in friendly territory. So long as we weren't sneaking around in civilian clothing, the Protestants loved what we were doing. If we were patrolling in uniform, they would stop and chat and the contrast was striking. Within twenty yards, you could move from a Catholic-controlled area to another that was Loyalist. In the first, they would want to kill you and in the second, they would make you a cup of tea. I have been dragged into the pub and had beers forced on me in Loyalist areas. That was the difference and the boundaries between those two very different worlds were sometimes just two or three streets. Some Catholic or Protestant areas were big but some were tiny. Either way, if you were caught in the wrong one, you would die.

It was a surreal situation and compounded by the fact that the British government refused to declare it a war because it was on their back doorstep and would be bad for their image, trade and tourism. I am interested in history and I read up on the Troubles and the background to it all. My conclusion? It was a shit-pie for everybody over there.

I'm a believer in the old adage that there are always three sides to an argument: there is my side, your side and the truth. That's what we had in Northern Ireland, which was a terrible situation, compounded by people using religion to suit their own aims. You had the nationalistic attitude of the Catholics clashing with the defend-at-all-costs status of the Protestants. I did feel empathy for both sides. I had a lot of respect for the Irish Republican Army as well because you have to respect your enemy and they were very professional in certain circumstances, though not in others, but the way the people treated each other there was really hard to swallow. You had to push that to the back of your mind and get on with your job because no one could make that right and, to an extent, it is still happening now, even in peacetime.

There are versions of the "Troubles" going on all over the world. It happened in the former Yugoslavia and in Burma (now Myanmar) and in Syria. If we hadn't sent the Army into Northern Ireland, I have no doubt that there would have been ethnic cleansing from one side or the other.

When I left the Northern Ireland I have just described, you might think I was glad to see the back of it, but the truth was actually very different. I absolutely loved it there. I missed the excitement, the buzz, the camaraderie and being in a team with really professional operators, where everyone was doing something useful and meaningful. When people are pushed to the limit you often see the best of them, and admittedly sometimes the worst, and there was a massive team spirit and resilience. It is always good to see everybody up their game when confronted with adversity, and that was what I really liked about being there.

The only thing on my mind from the day I left was how I could get back there. I was heading off to my next posting to the new territories in Hong Kong with the intention of getting straight back to Northern Ireland as soon as I could. There was just one problem. It was something beyond my control and it cost me any chance I might have had of getting back to Northern Ireland. My marriage imploded.

BACK TO HAUNT ME

M y falling-out with the SIB establishment before I left for Northern Ireland would come back to haunt me. I soon found out that they did not forgive or forget.

In 1991, I was sent to Hong Kong, which was still under British rule, for a posting with the Gurkhas at Shek Kong, a small outpost on the Hong Kong–Chinese border. We supported these excellent Nepalese soldiers, who have served with the British since 1815, as they patrolled the border to prevent illegals from entering the country. I was part of the QRF (Quick Reaction Force) when a typhoon struck Hong Kong city. The police post was on a mountain right in the eye of the storm. It was a beautiful sight and a most surreal moment.

While I was out in Hong Kong, my marriage ended and I got divorced. Melanie and I married young and had kids early. At times, I felt like we had become more like brother and sister than man and wife and, looking back, I think we loved each other but weren't in love. It became clear that neither of us was getting what we wanted from the marriage.

I felt that I wasn't getting the support or the affection that I needed and Melanie didn't see a lot of me for much of the time, which must have been difficult for her. I was often away doing courses or working irregular hours, so she was left to cope with the kids on her own.

There was no dramatic falling-out; we just grew apart and decided to split up. There comes a point where, for your own sanity, you have to put yourself first, and there was a period when I suppose I was the bastard in her eyes, but it wasn't easy for me either. I can remember a period of about two months or so when I honestly did not have a penny to my name because all of my money had gone to support my soon-to-be ex-wife and kids. There I was, approaching thirty, and I had to live on the base and eat there to save money but I still had nothing left.

Melanie left Hong Kong to return home. I had the kids until she found a place to live, then I had to fly back with them to drop them off with their mum. Those were difficult times, particularly when I packed up their stuff, and I really missed them when I had to return to Hong Kong.

These days, we are fine with one another. I get along okay with Melanie when we speak to or see one another. Everyone met up at my daughter's wedding and it was all civilized with no bitterness, which is good. Back then, our breakup had an immediate and lasting impact on my military career though.

The Army had a policy that if you were going through a marriage breakup you couldn't do certain roles for eighteen months in case your mental health wasn't good. They were being overcautious and, for someone like me, eighteen months twiddling your thumbs in a boring role felt like an eternity. It prevented me from returning to Northern Ireland where I was meant to finally join the FRU (Force Research Unit) and, when I factored in my lack of promotion, it made me start to seriously wonder about my future and whether I even had one in the forces.

I got a crap posting at Donnington near Telford and I didn't want to be there. It was an Operational Field Unit on exercises but it wasn't busy. The OC (officer commanding) created insane amounts of needless work. Some of the men hadn't had any days off in months. I had completed my sergeant courses in Northern Ireland, was due to be made up to sergeant permanently and the OC was a big fan of mine, so I thought I would be looked after but it didn't work out that way. Instead, they stopped my promotion, again. Despite getting nothing but A1 reports over the years, the promotion board rejected me for the third time. It was all politics and I realized I was never going to be promoted there. I didn't have a future in the military anymore. I had been a Red Cap for ten years but I instinctively knew my time was up.

The unit I was in at the end was run by a major I got on well with at first, but he turned into a right idiot after a while. Three-quarters of his unit had PVR'd (pre voluntary release), which meant they were asking to leave the Army, because of the way he was. The morale of the unit was so low and it felt like the very worst place to be. It was so bad that I even went back to the SIB temporarily because they were short of manpower and needed help for a while. I actually thought about going back to them permanently but that wouldn't have ended well, so, in the end, I felt that I was left with no choice but to leave the Army and I put my papers in.

The OC changed his opinion of me massively as soon as I PVR'd. Things went badly from then on and it was not a nice time for me. The way my military career ended left a very bitter taste in my mouth and it was a shame that this was all mostly down to one individual. I saw some terrible sights in that unit, including serious bullying and men crying over it. It was just an awful place to be.

Thankfully, I had bought a house in Newport near Donnington and was living away from the base there. When I left, the process was that you got some leave and the chance to do a couple of courses to prepare you for civilian life but that was about it. It's not like it is today. You got very little help when you left the military back then.

I worked out my time and went back in to sign my final report, which I really didn't want to do but I had no choice. One of the senior non-commissioned officers started giving me shit about how he had never liked me since the day I first came there and I thought, *What a cock.* I said, "Who the fuck are you anyway?" and he soon shut up. We then went in to the see the OC and he had two sergeants in there with him, which was unusual. They were both friends of mine but I could see in their faces that they were thinking, *Please don't kick off, Lee*—not that I was known for kicking off but you could tell they were worried that something was going to happen that day. The OC said, "There is my final report on you, Sansum." And he slid it toward me so I could read it then sign.

He was obviously expecting a row and I knew it would be a shit report from him, so I said, "I don't even want to read it. Give me the pen." And I looked him in the eye as I signed it.

I found out quite recently that the OC asked those two sergeants to be in there with him because he was scared of me. He told them he thought I was "going to do him," which was pathetic.

The process of leaving the Army was a really bad one for me and it was the same for a lot of the guys who left that unit around then. Up until that point, I hadn't really considered going. The Army was my life and I was planning to stay in it forever. Ironically, just before I left there were a load of redundancies. I could have applied for that and left with a shitload of money but I didn't go for it. Then, within three or four months, there was me PVR-ing and getting absolute fuck-all for leaving.

OUT IN THE COLD

Ironically, when I left the Army in 1994, I was determined I wouldn't work in security like so many other former military men. I also didn't want to return to the only other thing I knew. Instead of sheet metal work, I opted for something completely different. I got a job as an insurance salesman for the Prudential. It was quite a contrast from my life before and since but I was good at it. Pretty quickly, I became the top sales guy for my area and I made quite a lot of money. There was just one problem: I absolutely hated it. I was so bored by how quiet my life had become that, after a while, I had to admit it obviously wasn't for me, so I quit.

I then went back to the life I had known before the Army and got some work in a sheet metal factory in Telford. The manager there gave me a trial and showed me a load of jobs that needed doing. He said, "If you can weld these, there is about four weeks' work here for you." On day one, I made a load of jigs up. A jig is made of metal and they are a sort of template to help you with the job. Once my jigs were done, I did that four weeks' worth of work in just a couple of days. It made me unpopular with my new fellow workers but the company was so impressed they offered me a manager's job and I took it. There was a problem here, too, though. In the military, I had been around highly trained people with specialist expertise. That spoiled me for working in an ordinary place in the outside world. The people I was working with now seemed a bit dead to me in comparison.

I was thirty-three years old and finally starting to realize that a normal working environment was not for me. Luckily, I had a good contact in Paul Handley-Greaves. He was ex-military and had just taken over the running of Mohamed Al-Fayed's security team. He'd sacked a bunch of guys because he thought they had the wrong attitude, even some "Blades," the nickname given to former SAS men because of the dagger on their insignia. They might have been elite soldiers but some had bad reputations or massive egos, so Paul got rid of them and he needed good replacements.

I met Paul in Northern Ireland where he was serving as an officer and we knew each other well. We spoke on the phone and it wasn't a long conversation. He said, "Look, Lee, I've let a load of guys go and I want you on the team." Then he invited me to come down to London to visit Al-Fayed's HQ in Park Lane. I figured, why not?

When I got there, I saw a bunch of people doing interviews and those tests where they analyze your handwriting, but I didn't have to do any of that. Paul just said, "I know you and what you can do. If you want this, Lee, you're in."

Very wealthy businessmen like Mohamed Al-Fayed can easily make enemies. They and their family members can be at risk of kidnap for ransom or even assassination, if they have upset the wrong people from the wrong countries. That's why they need bodyguards, and Al-Fayed had a big team of them. He had fallen out with a few serious people in different parts of the world as his business empire grew and had received death threats.

He wasn't very popular in the UK either, at least with anyone associated with the government that he eventually helped to bring down. He exposed the MPs involved in the cash-for-questions scandal, Tim Smith and Neil Hamilton, which ruined their careers when Al-Fayed revealed he had been paying them to ask parliamentary questions on his behalf. He then provided evidence that destroyed Jonathan Aitken's libel case against the *Guardian,* sending the former cabinet minister to prison for perverting the course of justice. Al-Fayed could well have made some powerful enemies in the process.

All new members of the security team had to spend a couple of weeks in the Park Lane offices to get to know the layout of the buildings and their escape routes. There were maps to learn, too, with the location of all the security cameras marked on them. We would watch Al-Fayed on CCTV as he walked round Harrods, to get used to his routine. We had to know it by heart and that included all the places the family liked to hang out in, including bars, restaurants and museums.

The first time I saw Al-Fayed in person was when he stepped out of the lift in the foyer at Park Lane. He was pre-warned by Paul that there would be a new guy there so he wouldn't be alarmed to see a face he didn't recognize. He just flicked his eyes in my direction then walked away. I already knew that if he didn't like the look of you for any reason, you would be gone. That was fair enough because it was his team and they were responsible for his life, so he had to be 100 percent happy with it.

The next time it was me that opened the doors for him but I didn't say anything more than, "Good morning, sir."

He saw a bit more of me when I went up to the office, but it was months before he actually spoke to me. He probably thought there was no point getting to know new people in case they didn't stay long.

I worked at Park Lane for a few months and did a week on then a week off. It was seven days a week when you were working and you lived in, so you were there twenty-four hours a day. The security team had its own accommodation built into one of the residences in 55 Park Lane, which wasn't bad, considering that a one-bedroom flat there will set you back one and a half million quid these days and some of the bigger apartments fetch more than five million.

The Harrods Holdings company was based in three connected buildings, which was really handy because we could go from one building to the other through secret doors without anyone knowing. Some looked like doors but with no handles. Others you would never know were doors at all. You had to radio the ops room to unlock them remotely and they would ping open for you. If you tried to carry out surveillance on us, you would not know where we might come out. It meant Al-Fayed could enter and leave without being spotted.

We had counter-measures designed to reduce risk, including bulletproof windows and blast curtains and there were four armored Mercedes cars all with the same spec, so we could use them as decoys. We even had Al-Fayed masks; one of the lads would put one on and sit in the back of the car. Anyone watching would think it was the man himself leaving the building. It might sound paranoid but that is pretty standard for close protection at this level.

Our main aim was to avoid any potential threat. We regularly used counter-surveillance drills to identify any vulnerabilities.

We would ask ourselves, if we wanted to hit the principal, how would we do it? Then we would conduct exercises designed to block any surveillance of us. I'd be thinking, *If I wanted to watch our place, where would I look from?* Once I'd identified a spot, we'd check it out. If it was a tree, for example, we would look for signs that people had climbed it, like trampled grass or obvious tracks trodden into the ground. Were there cigarette butts that had been carelessly dropped by someone or vehicle tracks nearby? If it was a building, we would observe it and watch for watchers. This was important work because most assassinations are preceded by a long period of surveillance.

The basic principles never changed, whether we were at home in London or abroad in a hostile environment. That level of security isn't cheap and it must have cost Al-Fayed well over a million a year back then. The money was spent on a team of approximately fifty men and some women.

From day one, I absolutely loved the job. I think it was the responsibility and the fact that I was working with some exceptional people. They were all former military, with ex-SAS and SBS, some Paras, Marines, Special Branch and people who had worked for MI5. These guys were all experts. The money was pretty decent too. I was on about £40,000 a year and that was twenty-six years ago, so it would be the equivalent of about £80,000 now and we only worked six months of the year because of the week-on, week-off system. Some of the guys did other jobs when they were free but I spent most of my time training to improve my martial arts. When I wasn't doing that I was out drinking, meeting women and generally having a good time.

It wasn't long before I was asked to go and protect Al-Fayed's family at Barrow Green Court, the mansion he owned near Oxted in Surrey. Dodi, his eldest son, lived in Park Lane but the rest of the family, including his wife, Heini; his other sons, Omar and Karim; and daughters, Jasmine and Camilla, stayed there. I got on with his boys and I think it helped that Omar, at eight, was around the same age as my own son, Damon.

Their daily security was a big job because the place they lived in was massive. There was an outer perimeter and if you breached that it would ping before you got to the next level and so on, so we would see you coming. The family had high expectations for everything and that included their security. Their lifestyle was obviously lavish and I could see that this affected some of the guys who looked after them. Maybe they resented Al-Fayed's wealth but you cannot have an opinion about the principal you are guarding. You have to stay completely neutral about them or it becomes a distraction. The bodyguard can never become bigger than the client.

Heini hated having security but got on well with me. Their daughter Jasmine was around sixteen or seventeen back then and, like any teenager, she found security annoying and rebelled against it. I could tell this was going to be a problem, so I told her, "Just tell me if you are going to run away, Jasmine, because I'll resign right now if you are. I am not having your dad sacking me because of you." And she never gave me any trouble at all after that.

Omar was demanding, too, when he was little, but no more than any young boy, and he reminded me of Damon, so we got on fine. He even added me on Facebook a few months ago and we exchanged messages. He said he wanted to thank me for everything I had done for him, which was really nice.

Al-Fayed has been accused of being a bully, but I just saw him as a forthright person. Every sergeant in the Army who shouted at me to turn me into a better soldier could be called a bully by today's standards. By now, Al-Fayed trusted me completely and knew me well. Well enough, in fact, to be alarmed when he saw me back at HQ and he questioned why I was not at his home in Surrey, guarding his family. I was going up an escalator in Harrods when he spotted me and barked, "What the fuck are you doing here, Lee? You need to keep looking after my boys." Then he turned to the Alpha team leader and told him, "If anything happens to them, I'll cut your balls off." He was joking about that . . . I think.

I liked Al-Fayed because there was no side to him and he was the same all the time. He had high standards and you knew that if you fucked up, you would be fired but I had no problem with that. We used to close down his office at night and do an electronic sweep for bugs. On one occasion, an ex-infantry guy on the team went in to do it. You had to unplug the five phones, each with different lines; they were color-coded, so you could identify the phone that went back into each slot. It was important that Al-Fayed knew which phone went to which extension. But this bloke couldn't be arsed so he just plugged them back in and got them mixed up. The next day he was sacked.

We had another former SBS guy on the team and I went out in a car with him. I was astonished when he asked me to slow down and pull over because he was suffering from motion sickness! How that guy managed to get through the Special Boat Service's selection process, which I assume must involve a fair bit of time in flimsy boats on choppy waters, but couldn't cope with driving around London is beyond me. He had to go too.

One of the jobs of the residential security team at Oxted was to lock down the whole place at night. There were thirty doors to check and twenty corridors to patrol looking for signs of anyone trying to force entry. That could take an hour but it was an essential job. The lads manning the ops room could see what you were doing on the cameras and I watched one new guy as he went along the corridors without checking that the doors were locked because he couldn't be bothered. I went to Paul and said this guy has to go.

It is surprising when men who have been part of British military units prove to be crap at close protection duties, but it's all to do with passion for the job. Close protection is different to asset protection. You need to have an ingrained desire to look after people or you won't be any good at it. If you hire guys who have no passion and just do it for the money, you end up with a shit operator. When men leave the rigid discipline and hierarchy of the military behind, they often revert to who they were before they signed up. If they were lazy or dishonest before they joined, they often go back to that mindset once they are out. When people are in the armed forces, they are under massive pressure. Some of it is peer pressure because their mates and colleagues rely on them to do the right thing and they are also under orders, so when they leave it is a game changer. Suddenly, they are expected to think for themselves, with nobody checking on them. When they are out, a lot of guys default to their old community standards. If there is no longer anyone chasing them and they have no fear of consequences, they act differently. But whatever the reason, those guys did not last with us. We only wanted the best because lives depended upon it.

I only came close to losing my job with Al-Fayed once and that had nothing to do with his security. I was in the ops room when I noticed a big bag full of women's clothes, so I asked what they were. I was told they were his daughter Jasmine's old dresses and they were being donated to the charity shop. I had to go into town anyway, so I said I would take them.

One of the girls on the team saw one of the dresses on the top of the bag in my car and she said how nice it was. "Take it and make a donation to the charity store," I told her. I then took the rest of the dresses and the women in the store were delighted with them all.

A few days later, one of the housekeepers walked in and asked, "Have Jasmine's dresses come back from the dry cleaners? She wants to wear one of them to her prom."

Holy shit! That bag of dresses was destined for the cleaner not the charity shop and I had donated them all. In a panic, I realized I had just given away the boss's daughter's favorite dresses and they were probably worth tens of thousands of pounds.

I phoned the lass on the team and ordered her to "get that fucking dress back here sharpish." Then I drove straight down to the charity shop, only to be told that most of Jasmine's dresses had already been sold. "You have to get them back for me!" I told them, and let's just say I urged them to get in touch with the new owners.

Somehow, we steadily managed to get them all back from their new owners and just in time for Jasmine's prom, so she never knew what had happened. Of course, I ended up out of pocket because I had to buy them all back from the charity shop. It was an expensive mistake but not as bad as being fired for losing them.

TOM AND SLY

Being part of Al-Fayed's team meant moving in the same circles as he did. His son Dodi was a film producer and there were often events at Harrods that involved world- famous people, including Hollywood film stars. My main aim was to keep everyone safe, so I had no time to be starstruck but close protection work means you end up spending a lot of time in proximity to some very well-known people. Their adoring fans could only dream of that kind of access.

In terms of Hollywood royalty, it didn't get much bigger than Tom Cruise and Nicole Kidman when they were a married couple back in the nineties. There has been a lot of negative stuff written in the newspapers about Cruise in particular, due to his belief in Scientology and tabloid reports that he has forbidden eye contact from extras and technicians on set, but the guy I met and looked after for a couple of days couldn't have been nicer. Nicole Kidman was lovely, too, and very beautiful. You can see why she is a movie star. Both of them were happy to chat about things. They are no longer a couple but more than twenty-five years later they are still both on the Hollywood A-list.

I met Goldie Hawn at Harrods, too, and talked with her for some time. Like most blokes my age, I was a little in love with her after seeing her star in *Private Benjamin.* Of course, there was no guarantee that the beautiful, funny woman you see on the screen would be pleasant in real life but she was lovely and very easy to talk to. When she heard that Mohamed's son Omar was close by, she came into the room to say hello but Omar was only little back then and he took one look at this movie star and was too shy to talk to her.

"Sorry," I told her, "he is only a small boy." And she was fine about it but I wonder if he remembers the day he met Goldie Hawn.

We were carrying out our usual duty of looking after Mr. Al-Fayed while there was a big book signing going on in Harrods. Pelé was in town but that didn't really affect us too much because he had his own security team with him and we never used the main doors anyway. Beneath the store there are secret tunnels that go right under the roads that we used as passageways to go in and out.

But as we returned to our cars, we saw the greatest footballer in the world coming toward us with his team, on their way into the store. We took one look at them and we all thought the same thing: *These guys are idiots.* They were wearing flash suits and impractical, patent-leather shoes with leather soles, which would have no grip if you had to run in them. Their jackets were too tight, so anyone observing them would know they had no weapons or radios. Nobody was carrying a man-bag either, so it was obvious they had no medical equipment with them.

Our opinion of them was correct. They got Pelé inside the store alright but there was a massive crush, with loads of people pushing to get to the great man, and they completely lost control of the situation. Our boss was out of harm's way but Pelé's team just seemed to collapse as they were pushed and jostled by the crowd and Pelé was pinned back. We couldn't allow Brazil's favorite son to be trampled to death in Harrods, so me and my mate went back in for him. He is not tiny by any means but at around five feet eight inches tall, he is not so big for a man who could leap like a salmon when he needed to score bullet headers.

By the time we parted the crowd and reached him, Pelé must have been worried because his team didn't have a clue what to do. He looked a bit confused when we appeared and took over. I told them all, "Lads, follow me. We are going to take you out of here." When you say something like that with enough authority people tend to follow you, particularly when they are worried about their own safety. It's psychology, really. They had all frozen but I looked like someone who was in control, so they complied and we got Pelé to safety.

It's amazing what you can get away with if you look and sound authoritative enough and recognize the power of a suit. Ever noticed how people treat you differently depending on what you are wearing? You get a lot more respect when you are dressed in a suit and tie than you do in a T-shirt and jeans.

Sylvester Stallone was a nice guy but he is another film star who is quite tiny in real life. Everyone knows that Tom Cruise is only five feet seven inches tall but they still expect the star of *Rocky* and *Rambo* to be a big man, even though he is only an inch or so taller than Cruise. Perhaps it is the tough-guy image or the muscles but when we saw him in St. Tropez it was quite a shock.

He was a good bloke, though, and never gave us any grief. While we were looking after him in France, word got out that he was in a store and there was a crush to get at him, so we had to take him out of there. I think Sly was panicking a bit but one of our guys told him, "Put your hand in the back of my belt and hold your girlfriend's hand and I will get you both through the crowd." He then used his eye contact and bulk to force his way through while Rambo followed, holding onto his belt.

If you have the correct posture and move with authority you can get through any crowd. They think you are police, and before they have worked out that you are not, you are gone. I did it once at Fulham FC with Al-Fayed's kids. There was a massive crowd and people were trying to get to them, even though they didn't know why or even who they were. The word got out that they were with the other club's directors. Someone must have seen the armored cars we arrived in and I knew we stood out dressed in suits. I'd said to the team this could get tricky and it did. Members of a crowd can get a shot of adrenaline and adopt tunnel vision without realizing it. The result is that, as they are watching who I am with, they are not seeing me. They lose hearing, too, with adrenaline and can't hear what I am saying either. When that happens, I can push them to one side and they won't see me do it. If I push their shoulder, I can spin them right round. If things get really bad, a well-aimed strike will drop them instantly in more serious situations.

If they are looking at you instead of the client, you can engage with them to get them back into what I call their adult-thinking brain, but you have to be authoritative. Barking, "Madam, you need to step back!" is an effective method. When someone addresses you like that in a commanding manner, your subconscious brain makes you think it's your dad, your teacher or a police officer that's talking to you.

People's brains are used to acting in a pre-planned way, which means you can use your voice as a weapon. I can confuse just by speaking loudly but with no signs of aggression in my posture or I can flip it and calmly say to a would-be attacker, "Listen, mate, I don't want to get blood on my clothes in here, so can we go outside?" or "Can you come closer to get away from the CCTV?", which will bemuse an aggressor because they are automatically wondering what you are planning to do to them if you don't want the CCTV to see it. You have to have balls to do this and you must say it with conviction and stay as cool as ice for it to be effective. It does work though. I have used that technique on a guy with a knife and even one man who killed someone with a shotgun shortly after I had a run-in with him, and I am still here.

You can apply psychology and use your voice and body language to good effect when you are off duty too. I was in New York visiting my brother and a group of us were on a night out. We walked by one of those bars that always has a massive line outside, where you have to queue for ages unless you are a celebrity. The women in our group really wanted to go inside and they said they would happily pay $100 each for a night there.

I said, "Give me fifty bucks each and I will get us in."

They handed over the money and everyone was dressed nicely, so I told them to wait off to one side, keeping a little distance between them and the club.

I walked up to the doorman at the head of this huge queue and said, "Hi, mate. I was in here last week." I indicated our party. "You can clearly see who I am with but please don't draw attention to them." As if they were very big celebrities indeed. Then I asked, "Can you look after us like you did last time?" I then shook his hand, gave him the $350 I had collected and told him we were only going in for an hour. He smiled and opened up the velvet rope; I beckoned everyone over and we all walked in.

Our trickiest client was Jean-Claude Van Damme. I'd worked with him before while guarding Al-Fayed and he was what you might describe as difficult. Then, years later, I got a call to ask if I could offer close protection for him while he was launching a martial arts documentary in several cities across the UK. I could not be there in person this time but I had a couple of good guys I could put onto a job like that and the money was good for all of us.

Unfortunately, Jean-Claude was a bit difficult on that job too. It was so bad that I got a call from the guy who was supposed to be protecting him. He was ex–RAF Regiment and those guys are known as "rock apes" in military circles. In Aden in 1952, two RAF Regiment officers decided to go hunting for apes. One of them accidentally shot the other and wounded him, explaining later that, in the dim light of evening, his friend "looked just like a rock ape." All it took was one careless idiot with a gun to land an entire regiment with a derogatory nickname that has lasted for generations. Anyway, this guy had finally had enough of Van Damme and I listened to him with increasing alarm as he told me, "Lee, I am going to go back into that room to smash his face in."

Van Damme might be a martial arts expert but he is a tournament fighter and not on the same level as the men doing his close protection. There was a very real chance he might get knocked out, then none of us would get paid. Worse, I'm not sure many people would hire close protection from bodyguards who were known to occasionally beat up their clients. I told my guy to calm down while I talked him out of killing Jean-Claude. As soon as I got off the line, I called Jack, the other guy on that job, and told him to get over to that room sharpish to keep an eye on things. So Van Damme had a bodyguard and, that day, the bodyguard had one too. What a farce. I suspect Jean-Claude never knew how close he came to getting a good hiding.

CHANGE

If it had not been for the car crash in Paris, I probably would have ended up in America, as part of the Al-Fayed security team tasked with looking after Diana and Dodi. Now that they were gone, everything was up in the air and everyone was affected by the accident. It was a really intense time. We were all very upset about what had happened and the family were grieving. Some of the security team had already moved on. The London operation was a horrible place to be in at that time.

When I wasn't there, I was living on my own in Baxenden, a village in Lancashire probably best known as the home of Holland's pies. I was in a bad relationship at the time, which didn't help, and it soon went toxic, so that was another reason why I wanted to get away.

So when I heard that the security guy at the St. Tropez estate was leaving, I jumped at the chance of replacing him for a while. I went out there for four weeks and it was just what I needed. By then, the summer was over and it was a quiet time in St. Tropez. I had free run of the villa complex, a four-acre site with a thirty-bedroom estate. A winding road took you for about half a mile from the beach up the hill to the main house, which was inside a gated enclosure. As well as the main house, there were a couple of guest houses, a fisherman's cottage and the accommodation for up to twenty security guys, who weren't needed at this point because the family weren't using it. The place was virtually empty and mostly locked up.

I had my own quarters and even a sun terrace on the roof. I just had to hang out there and keep an eye on the place to make sure everything was looked after. The housekeeper and his wife were still there but I hardly saw them because it was such a big site. He booked everyone in and out at the front gate, which was not manned when the family were absent. It was done by cameras and an intercom. The only people coming in and out, apart from us, were some local French builders who were creating an underground luxury spa next to the disco. I would say hello to them each morning but they usually finished their day early then were on the piss, so I didn't see that much of them.

I didn't have much to do really but I kept myself busy and tried to be useful. I cleaned the pools and watered the plants in the greenhouse, I checked the boathouse and walked the perimeter, making sure everything was as it should be. I had some monitors and cameras and there were alarms but it was so quiet and nothing ever happened. The place was almost deserted and, because it was gated, everything was locked up at night. I just had to walk round last thing to make sure all was in order.

I had the use of a car so I could go into town and have a walk round then stop for a coffee. No one was there because St. Tropez is dead during the off-season. All the nightclubs and most of the restaurants were shut; it is a surreal place when it is deserted. I was used to seeing a display of wealth, with rich people sitting on the back of enormous boats, publicly eating and drinking while everyone else gawped at them. St. Tropez right then was like Blackpool in the wintertime. Everything was shut up and waiting for next year.

To keep fit, I would go for a run around the perimeter of the estate and we had some weights I could use. I rigged up a punch bag, so I could continue my karate training and I could go for a swim. I had everything I could possibly need at that point and look back fondly on the time when I was the Thomas Magnum of St. Tropez, like the fictional character in *Magnum PI*, who lived on a rich man's estate in Hawaii. All in all, it wasn't a bad life for a while.

Because it was so quiet, I had plenty of time to reflect and think about my future, and that's exactly what I needed. The sudden, accidental deaths of Diana and Dodi left me considering my own mortality and got me wondering what I really wanted out of my life.

I wasn't planning on leaving but I did need a change of some kind. I loved working for the Al-Fayeds. I really liked the family and had a good relationship with all of them, including the boss, and I was one of the few security men who could have a chat with his wife. I think Heini was taken aback by that. She probably thought all of the security guys were just door-kickers but I was interested in some of the same stuff she was and we would even talk about the flowers in her greenhouse.

While I was looking after the St. Tropez estate, I kept in touch with the guys in the ops room back in London. That's how I found out that the guy looking after Al-Fayed's Scottish estate was leaving too. He was an ex-Marine and was planning to come down and work at Harrods. I started to think it might be a good idea if I went the other way.

Rosehall in Sutherland is a tiny hamlet in the middle of a 26,000-acre estate owned by Al-Fayed. Getting away there seemed like a very attractive proposition, particularly when I added my son into the equation. My ex-wife, Melanie, had told me she was concerned about Damon. He was only ten years old but she was finding it hard to control him and thought that he might need a father's influence. I wondered if maybe it was time for his dad to play a more active part in his life.

I decided to ask for the job in Scotland and take Damon up there with me. I spoke to Paul Handley-Greaves, the head of security, and put in a request to go but he refused. "The boss will never let you go," he said. "He will want you here in London." I was supposed to take that as a compliment and drop the matter, but I wasn't going to give up yet. I put my case to him and explained about my family situation. I knew that Paul was leaving soon, so I pleaded with him, "Will you do me this one favor, as my goodbye present from you, and let me go there? The boss won't even know about it for a while, and by the time he does realize, I will be up there and I'll be settled."

"For fuck's sake, Lee," he said, exasperated with me. Then he finally gave in. "Okay, you can go."

I was delighted and relieved. I borrowed a Luton van and loaded up all of my gear. I rented out my house in Baxenden and drove north, picking up Damon from his mother's on the way, then we headed for our new home, which was four hundred miles away, in a village slap-bang in the middle of the Highlands. On a clear day, you could see both the west and east coasts of Scotland from the top of the mountain on Al-Fayed's land.

The contrast between our old lives and our new one was immediately obvious, but we loved the wild, open spaces. We lived in a cottage on the estate and I spoilt Damon rotten. He went to the local school, Rosehall Primary, which could not have been more different from his old one. There were only nine kids in the entire school, for a start. I would drive him up there every day in my Land Rover and I always helped the school when they had trips by taking some of the kids along in my car.

While he was getting a decent education at the school, I set about teaching him the sort of life skills you don't learn in a classroom. I taught Damon martial arts in the front room of the cottage; he learned to fish in the river and I showed him how to build dams. I even taught him to drive the Land Rover. Damon could barely reach the pedals but he just about managed it and we were safe because he learned to drive it on wide open spaces. We had so much flat land on the estate that used to be flooded by the River Cassley and you could drive for miles across pasture on the flood plain. I didn't just teach Damon how to drive to boost his confidence; it was mainly so he would be safe. We were on a huge estate and if something ever happened to me while we were miles from anywhere, at least he could get back. In the end, he became quite a good driver at the age of ten.

I taught Damon how to use a shotgun and a rifle and we would shoot clays together with the locals. He liked his football and the school had a pitch, so I scheduled certain nights a week to go there and teach him how to play. I was a decent footballer and could perhaps have gone professional at one stage so it was good to pass that on to him.

Damon was a good kid but he was a very shy boy when we arrived there and he wouldn't even go into a shop and ask for stuff. Part of my mission as his dad was to show him how to talk to people, so I started getting him to do things for himself, like go into a shop and ask for something, and when we went out for a meal, which we did often, I would make sure he ordered his own dinner. Slowly and gently, I brought him out of himself and it was great to see the change in him as he became more confident.

Just across from my house there was a pub in the tiny village and we would walk there most nights for a meal together and I would have a couple of pints. We were a father and son but also a lot like friends and I treated him like a friend. We had a really good relationship and he went everywhere with me. It was the most amazing father and son time, and he learned a lot. I am so glad I took him with me. It was a very different world from St. Tropez or the London properties but I loved it.

Although my main responsibility was obviously security, I would liaise with the local community on Al-Fayed's behalf too. I saw myself as an extra pair of hands and I was happy to help anyone out. I assisted the farmers if they needed anything doing, including dipping the sheep and even artificially inseminating them, which wasn't exactly in my job description. I assisted the deer stalker and sometimes went out shooting with him, and I helped him with the deer culling, which had to be done every year to maintain the right population numbers and prevent overgrazing.

I'd help the high-net-worth individuals, who were guests during the hunting and fishing season, if they needed something and I would walk the land and just check that everything was as it should be. I'd drive out to make sure the deer fencing was intact and I would go up to the salmon fishery to see if they were okay. I was pretty much left alone to do whatever I wanted to but I kept myself busy and lent a hand wherever I could.

If Al-Fayed needed anything, he knew I was up there and I was his eyes and ears on the estate. When he visited his castle, near Tain, about thirty miles away, which was the family residence, he would usually come up to Rosehall and ask me what was going on. He trusted me and knew he could call on me at any time if he needed anything. He got peace of mind out of me being there and I really enjoyed the freedom I was given.

I used to come down to Al-Fayed's castle once a week for a meeting with the rest of the lads on the security team, so I could see everyone and have a brew and a catch-up. One week, some members of the Guinness family were due to fly in, with Al-Fayed's second in command, Mark, staying at the Inveroykel Lodge, a large holiday home in the Highlands owned by Al-Fayed, but the team was shorthanded and they didn't have anyone to go to the airport to pick them up. I didn't usually do that sort of thing but I offered to help them out. It did not seem like a very big decision at the time but it was one that completely changed my life.

I drove to the airport in a minibus to pick everyone up, but the flight was delayed. Inverness airport was really tiny at the time, and while I was waiting for them, I spotted a woman sitting close by. She was very good-looking and dressed in a suit but she also looked really fit and healthy, as if she had done a lot of training, and that intrigued me. I wondered if perhaps she was a swimmer or something.

When the flight was delayed even further, I went to buy a coffee and we bumped into each other at the kiosk. She asked me if I knew what was wrong with the plane as she was waiting for someone. We got chatting and I asked her where she lived. She told me she had a place in Forres, and worked at the nearby college, in Elgin.

At this point in my life, I was absolutely not looking for a relationship. I had just come out of a toxic one and, though I was still seeing women, I did not want anything serious with anyone, but this woman intrigued me. When we spoke, I thought she was an absolute firecracker, but when the plane finally landed, I still hadn't got her name.

Mark arrived with the Guinness family members in tow and I had to drive off with them but I couldn't leave it at that.

"Mark," I said, "I know this is totally unprofessional . . ."

"What is it, Lee?" he asked suspiciously.

"You see that woman over there?" I pointed her out. "I just need to go and ask her name."

Thankfully, Mark loved that. He smiled. "Go on then."

I walked up to her and said, "Excuse me, I feel bad but I didn't ask you your name?" She told me it was Kate. Since I already knew where she worked, I now knew I could get in contact with her if I wanted to.

I went back home and thought about it for a few days then called the college in Elgin and spoke to the receptionist. I'm not ashamed to say that I used my training and my special investigation interrogation skills to get everything I needed out of that unsuspecting woman. Next, I bought a postcard with a giraffe on it and wrote a message to Kate. It said, "I am the guy you met at the airport and here is my number. I would like to give you a call and I am just letting you know."

A few days after that, I called Kate and we got chatting. That first call lasted about an hour and we talked again soon after that. I really liked her already because I had never met a woman with such contagious energy. She was so honest and open and I found it really refreshing. Kate had no agenda and was just completely confident and transparent.

Next, I went to a florist and said, "I want you to send some flowers and a George Michael DVD to this lady," and I gave them Kate's details.

The florist said, "We don't do that."

But I wanted it to be perfect, including the romantic songs on the DVD, so I pleaded, "What do you mean, you don't do that? You've got to do that. Look, I'll pay you anything you want. I just need you to walk out to the shop, get the DVD, wrap it up and send it with the flowers."

I must have been persuasive because she said, "Go on then."

I then told Kate that I was coming to see my cousin who lived in Elgin, which I wasn't, but it was a good excuse to ask her out for a drink and she said yes. That went well, so she came down to see me at Rosehall. We had the most amazing time there and started seeing each other regularly.

Eventually, in the summer of 1999, we went to Ibiza for a holiday together. After that, we realized that we could no longer live apart. By now, Kate had her own flat so Damon and I could move in with her but I wouldn't be able to continue my job with the Al-Fayed team from that distance. I would have to hand in my notice.

Damon also played a part in my decision to leave. Al-Fayed had come up to Rosehall and met Damon and taken a shine to him. Being a generous man, he bought him a stack of stuff in the local shop, then Damon was invited to the castle to play with Al-Fayed's sons, Omar and Karim, and he got on well with them both. Al-Fayed then asked me to come back down to Oxted to guard his boys but I explained I couldn't do that because of Damon, who was now settled in Scotland and his school. The boss offered a solution, which involved me bringing Damon with me. A house would be provided and Damon would move to a new school. It was generous of Al-Fayed to make that offer but it worried me. I didn't think it was a good idea for Damon to be exposed to that kind of wealth at an impressionable age. His mates would be the children of billionaires. Damon was just a normal kid. I wanted him to stay that way. The trouble was that you did not say no to the boss once he had an idea in his head, so I decided it was the right time to go.

I put my notice in and left the Al-Fayed security team, then we went to live with Kate in her flat in Forres. It was a big move for me and a massive change. I was thirty-seven years old and about to start an entirely new chapter in my life with Kate. Looking back, it's amazing to think that it would never have happened if I hadn't volunteered to pick someone up from the airport. We are still together, more than twenty years later, and very happily married with three great kids. We have been through a hell of a lot together too. That airport run was a real sliding doors moment for me. Who knows where I would be right now if that flight had landed on time?

Already winning karate titles, aged eighteen, back in 1980.

It was a proud day for me when I became a Red Cap—wearing the "depot recruit of the week" sash.

Making a comeback and winning the silver medal at the World Association of Kickboxing Organizations (WAKO) world championship in Villach, Austria, 2009.

With Princess Diana in St. Tropez just one month before she died. I got to know the princess and thought highly of her.

On a mission in Misrata, Libya, in 2014, protecting diplomats during meetings with the militia. The scud missile launcher was shot up and abandoned during the civil war.

Training on the shooting range in Somaliland was challenging and hazardous. You did not stand in front of these guys while they were holding Kalashnikovs.

Keeping order wasn't easy. One guy was disrespectful and wouldn't listen. He ended up with broken ribs.

The highly poisonous carpet viper that killed one of our men.

New recruits rarely knew how to handle a weapon. This guy used the stock of his Kalashnikov to carry a water bottle, which would have severely hampered him if he ever needed to fire it.

Leaving Somalia in a hurry. Our escape was like something out of that film *The Wild Geese*.

A desperate situation in Libya, 2014. We were sure we were all going to die.

Libya again in 2016. My personal ammo: twelve 30-round mags for my M4. At least we had enough ammunition this time.

Thousands converged at the Libya-Tunisia border, desperate to reach safety, and then the shooting started.

At the HALO Trust. Diana supported the mine-clearing charity. I was there years later, teaching their guys how to survive in hostile conditions.

Bodyguard to Alex Salmond during the Scottish independence referendum, 2014.

Still fighting! This time it's just a demo and no one got hurt.

With my son Damon, a double medal winner with the GB Olympic taekwondo team.

A guest of the Indian government when I was President of the World Martial Kombat Federation (WMKF). With my rock, Kate, at the Taj Mahal, by the bench where Princess Diana once sat for a famous photograph.

Training the Saudi Arabian military in Taif, in 2019. Avoiding the war zones these days.

On the runway at former dictator Colonel Gaddafi's private terminal at the military airport in Tripoli; the only place left where you could fly in and out of Libya in 2016, during the second civil war.

Relaxing in the garden of my Highland home.

Tooled up before going out on a mission. Carrying an M4 on a
rifle sling and my Glock. On the ground: my helmet and bags
containing a 48-hour survival kit, which included a passport,
money, protein snacks, clothing, spare mags, first aid kit, mobile
and sat phones, as well as a Gerber multitool knife.

LOSING EVERYTHING

Like any father, I was a little nervous about Damon meeting Kate for the first time, but I needn't have worried. They got on brilliantly right from the beginning. At the time, we thought Kate would never be able to have children but she liked kids and from the outset she loved Damon as if he were her own child. They instantly bonded and it was better than I ever could have hoped for. Kate has been there throughout Damon's life—attending his school evenings, helping him with his homework and mentoring him. I think he would acknowledge that where he is today is partly because of her. They have a very special relationship that means a lot to me.

Later, when Chamane was around sixteen years old, she came to live with us for a while too. The girls could see the quality of life Damon was having and how it was quite different from living in Blackpool so they wanted a bit of that for a while. Melanie wanted it for them, too, and she is grateful to Kate for the way she has looked after Damon as he was growing up.

When I left the Al-Fayed team and moved in with Kate, I didn't just jack in my job and hope that something else would magically come along. I had been thinking about my future for a while now. I'd thoroughly enjoyed working for the Al-Fayeds but I always knew it wouldn't last forever.

My plan involved raising a bit of money first then opening up my own business. I was going to have my own gym and fitness center and I had been planning this for a while, as far back as when I was on my own in St. Tropez. In preparation for this new direction, I took courses in fitness, nutrition and personal training and we started planning exactly what we were going to do.

Kate was already a fitness instructor in her spare time and she had a great business brain too. We found two vacant units next to each other and I decided to put a gym in one of them. I would teach karate and Kate would take fitness classes in the other but I needed the start-up money, so I checked out some well-paying security jobs abroad. The first was for a British bank who wanted a protection team to go out to Columbia to help their guys get money back that was owed to them. The second was in Algeria. It was pretty dangerous but not as bad as trying to reclaim money from people in the drugs capital of the world at the time. The Algeria job paid a grand a day so I could do a couple of months out there, earn sixty grand or so and come home with all of the capital needed to start up the business.

I had all the equipment sourced and ordered and I was just about to sign the lease when the job in Algeria suddenly fell through, leaving me with no money. We were stuck.

I had been in touch with a friend of mind, Steve Winsper, who ran a martial arts school. I called Steve and asked him how he was making money in his gym and he said it was actually through his karate, which seemed impossible to me back then but he told me he was making a decent sum. I asked if I could come down and see how he did it. So we drove 460 miles through the night, all the way down to Kidderminster, to see what he had going on, which was a really professional martial arts school. We came away thinking that we could do that.

With no start-up money, we went ahead anyway and began with our first karate class in a free room at the Mosset Tavern in Forres. Kate handled the PR and she wanted to describe me as "Princess Diana's former bodyguard," but I didn't want to do it because I wasn't comfortable putting it out there at the time. In the end, she made me realize it was the only angle we had that might interest the local media. How else could anyone know we were open for business? I finally agreed and it worked.

On our opening night, I looked outside and couldn't believe it. We had a massive queue of people all wanting to attend that first class. It stretched for more than fifty meters and I was overwhelmed by the numbers. In three years, we turned that karate school into a sizable business with a turnover of a third of a million pounds.

I did so much preparation for my classes and made them really good. We even got an invitation to put a class on at a big conference in Wales, involving some large martial arts companies and huge names in the industry. It went really well and lots of people came up to me afterwards to say how amazing it was, which was lovely, but that good feeling didn't last long. At a big meeting afterwards, everyone started talking about business and I was completely out of my depth. I had no idea what they were talking about and felt like a right idiot. Afterwards, I said to Kate, "Never again is that going to happen to me." And I meant it.

From that point, I made it my mission to find out about business. I went on marketing and sales courses and spent thousands educating myself on everything to do with business. I realized I'd had a very old-fashioned, working-class idea that money was dirty and, if you wanted it, you must be greedy. I knew that if I was ever going to succeed at this, I would have to change.

We grew our business until we had fourteen sites, turning it into a franchise operation because we couldn't be everywhere at once. Things went great for a while and it seemed like we had a really good thing going on. We started other businesses, including a hair and beauty salon and an armed forces resettlement company, then I invested in another business with an ex-RAF man, making martial arts suits and other clothing. I took out loans to invest in the various businesses but they were all doing well and my credit rating was high. Unfortunately, when things started to go wrong for us, they went very badly wrong indeed.

In a fairly short space of time, two of the couples who ran our centers backed out of plans to take them over as franchises. Both just walked away and I was left with a massive bill because I had just signed a ten-year lease on the building they were using. I had to sell that business on to someone else for a grand, though it was worth a hell of a lot more than that, just to escape the long-term liability for the rent. Those two incidents cost us around £150,000 a year in revenue. It hurt like hell after all those years of working really hard seven days a week, every week.

I had already resigned from the martial arts clothing business by that stage, but I didn't follow up and make sure the paperwork had been done to remove me formally as a director. A year after I left as a director of the company, I received a court summons demanding £20,000. I was still listed as a director on the records, so when the company eventually went bankrupt, I was liable for the whole £20,000.

Then the financial crash hit us in 2008 and the banks called in all of my loans and suddenly we were in very deep shit. I still had an old-fashioned attitude to money and debt, so trying to pay back all of my creditors seemed the right thing to do.

Actually, it was the wrong thing to do.

The strain was unbelievable. I had coped with difficult situations in the military but nothing like this because so much of it was beyond my control. We'd had a series of IVF treatments by now and Kate was heavily pregnant. She nearly lost our twin babies because of the stress.

The worst thing was how we very quickly went from being financially sound to having literally nothing. We kept a tin in the kitchen and put £20 in it at the start of the week—"Right, that is the money for all of our food for the week." That is how bad it got. We managed to keep the house because that was separate from all of this, but money to live on was virtually nonexistent.

I didn't think there was any alternative, until I mentioned our situation to someone with a background in business, who immediately asked me why we had not gone bankrupt. I was appalled at the notion but he assured me it was the only way out. He explained there was no way we would ever be free unless we declared ourselves bankrupt and started all over again and he was absolutely right. I just couldn't see it until he spelt it out for me. That was the only way this was ever going to end for us.

It was genuinely the most stressful period of my life, but despite everything that happened to us, I was never suicidal. I love Kate and my family too much for that but I will never forget the extraordinary stress levels we experienced.

Now we had to start all over again.

UNLAWFUL KILLING

Eleven years after Princess Diana's death, an inquest was finally held into it. The huge interest in both the princess and the circumstances of her death had led to endless speculation and a large number of conspiracy theories. The idea was to finally get to the bottom of it all in the hope that all of this might go away. The inquest was held in London in 2008 and it lasted for ninety-four days. I was called as a witness and I came down for it, booked into a hotel, put my best suit on and headed to the court.

I was walking up the street in London on the day I was scheduled to give evidence, when I noticed a crowd of people about two hundred meters ahead of me, outside the courthouse. Suddenly, the atmosphere changed and a number of them started to run in my direction. I turned to look over my shoulder to see who they were coming after but there was no one else there. I looked back and realized they were after me. It was a posse of reporters and they all wanted a word. At first, I didn't know what to do but I didn't want to speak to them like that, so I ran past and on into the court where I hid.

A court official who let me in was surprised that I hadn't anticipated the media scrum. "Were you not expecting this?" he asked me. But I had been away for years setting up the martial arts school. I had avoided reading the news about her and had underestimated the press interest in Diana, which hadn't waned despite all the intervening years. To be honest, I was a bit overwhelmed.

I was expecting some kind of briefing on how to conduct myself in the court but there was nothing. I walked by the public gallery and into the dock and I realized I didn't even know what to call the bloke in charge. Should I call him "sir" or "my Lord"? I had no idea, so I didn't call him anything.

I was on the back foot because I hadn't realized how big and serious this was going to be but I now made a point of making myself become really calm and collected until I felt okay with being in that situation. I have taught myself to do the same thing whenever I am faced with adversity and feel anxious. Mentally, I can take myself to a different place. It works when I am in dangerous situations or stressful ones, like at this inquest when it felt like the whole world was watching. I imagine that I have boxes in my head that are like big sea chests with locks on them. I take a moment to think about the thing that is frightening me and I say, "I don't need you right now." Then I unlock the chest and put that thing inside it, lock it up again and mentally throw away the key. I do that with anything that I don't need and I've been doing it for years. It helps to calm me and stops the adrenaline from flowing.

In a place like the court when it is busy or a bit crazy, I will head for the toilet and go into a cubicle before I am needed. I stand there for a moment and close my eyes, then I think about what it is that I am about to do. I look down on it as if from above and I think about everything else that is going on in the rest of the world, where so much big stuff is happening and people are dying. Then I come back to the thing I am about to do and I remind myself that it is nothing in the scheme of things. I tell myself that the only thing I have power over is me, then I lock away whatever it is that is stressing me. Finally, I come out of there and it is game on.

When my cross-examination started, I considered my responses and really thought about what I was going to say before I said it, which was the right thing to do because some of those lawyers really went for me. They had been through interviews I had given over the years and were picking up on every word I had said. They asked me what I really thought then and what I thought about it all now, years later. They demanded to know how I could be sure about exactly what Princess Diana had said to me so long ago. I kept calm and answered them to the best of my abilities and I made sure I did not get flustered by their questions or their tone, no matter how scathing or disbelieving they sounded. It was a stressful process but I told them everything I knew about Diana's state of mind, how we had seen former military guys following us on motorbikes and how we were used to being under surveillance with the Al-Fayed team even before she joined us. I did okay, but when it was over, I felt like I really needed a drink.

As I left the court, I went by a group of young lawyers who had gone in to watch proceedings. The woman they were with stopped me and said, "Mr Sansum, you were incredible in there and I have just told this group that you were a great example of how to give evidence in a very high-pressure situation." That obviously made me feel good about myself but she had no way of detecting the stress I was really under.

I had intended to go back to the hotel for a while before meeting a friend for a drink in the evening, but I called him and said, "Mate, you need to stop working and come now."

"Why? What have you been doing?"

When I told him I had been giving evidence at the Diana inquest, he couldn't believe it. He dropped everything, came to meet me and we headed straight for the pub and went on an epic bender. We got really pissed and ended up in Gaucho for a great meal and some very good wine. The next day I flew back to sleepy Moray, where no one had a clue what I had been doing.

∞

The inquest carried on and I watched the coverage with interest. During the proceedings, a clinical pharmacologist claimed that the blood tested after the crash was very likely not Henri Paul's and that the alcohol content of the blood samples was suspiciously consistent, considering they were taken from different parts of his body. To me, that discredits the claim that he was an alcoholic proven to be well over the limit for driving at the time of the accident, though the jury at the inquest disagreed, finding he had consumed alcohol before driving. The French doctor was not allowed to come over and give evidence at the inquest. A British doctor said it was not Henri Paul's blood but the French wouldn't send their people over to testify about what actually happened during the testing process. This just heightened my suspicion that it was all covered up. Maybe it is not in the public interest to know exactly how our security guys work, I get it. Once you start a story with a mistruth, it escalates and you have to tell one lie after another to keep up the pretense.

I still think the delay in getting the princess to the hospital was a major contributing factor to her death. If they had driven Diana straight there, who knows, she might have survived. Instead, they treated her at the scene. Maybe they had to do that initially, but why did it take them two hours to get her to the hospital after the accident? It made no sense to me. I could have carried her over my shoulder and gone on foot and still got there before they did.

There was an understandable focus on seat belts at the inquest and the fact that the people who died in the crash—Diana, Dodi and Henri Paul—were not wearing them. Only Trevor was and he survived, just. My initial reaction to the news of the crash had been to question how this could have happened—they were traveling in a robust car and I couldn't imagine how three people could have died on the streets of Paris like that. But then I saw the state of the vehicle. Later, when I learned they were not wearing seat belts, I began to understand why they didn't survive.

That shouldn't have happened. It was standard practice for the family to wear seat belts. It was an order sent down from the boss, in fact. Al-Fayed had a massive bee in his bonnet about seat belts, but we often battled with younger members of the family about them and the girls never liked to use them. Dodi, in particular, hated wearing seat belts, but I always insisted on it.

I first met Dodi when he walked out of the Hyde Park residence and climbed into the car, expecting to see Trevor Rees-Jones at the wheel, but Trevor couldn't be in his car that day and the boss had asked me to drive Dodi instead. I think he was worried he was about to be kidnapped at first because he had climbed into a car driven by someone he didn't recognize. His first instinct was to try to get out, but as soon as his arse touched the seat, the doors were locked. That was for his own safety. When the client is going in or out of their house and getting into a car parked outside, they are more vulnerable. Someone can attack at that point and may have been waiting nearby for the opportunity, so you cannot muck about. You want to be in that car and away as quickly as possible.

Dodi told me where he wanted to go, and even though I did not know him, I had to contradict him immediately. His father had given new instructions and the family were all going somewhere else, which Dodi wasn't pleased about. He would not put his seat belt on either, so I had to tell him that the car was not moving until he did. He wasn't happy about that either, so I suggested I could call his father to discuss it further. Immediately, he complied and we were able to get moving.

Even in hostile situations, you tell people to put a belt on, in case the car crashes or rolls. You are more likely to die like that when an enemy opens fire on you than from their bullets. Thankfully, I was wearing a seat belt when I had my bad car crash and hit that fence because I know I would not have walked away from the car otherwise.

For Dodi and Diana not to wear belts that night should have been as alien to them as forgetting to tie their shoelaces. If a bodyguard did forget to insist on it at the start of a journey, as soon as they had to drive fast they would think about it. I suppose it is possible that they didn't for some reason. That is the only explanation I can think of. Dodi was prone to that kind of darting around and whoever looked after him was always a bit knackered. He would be out late, he liked nightclubs and was sometimes up early the next morning and they never knew what he was going to do next.

In that sense, Dodi was perhaps a typical rich young man but he was also a very pleasant guy. He had a big party-boy image but inside he was just a quiet, nice bloke. He lived the life of a playboy but he was always trying to do the right thing and you could tell he wanted to make his dad proud of him. His father could be a ruthless businessman and that is how he built up his fortune, but Dodi wasn't like that. He didn't need to be because he already had money. Dodi behaved like any young man would want to in London, but he didn't do anything outrageous. He wasn't ignorant or arrogant; in fact, he was actually a bit shy.

There has been speculation in the press about his relationship with Diana not being very serious, but whenever I saw him with Diana, they were really friendly and affectionate toward one another. The guys on the security team all thought it was game on and would develop into a serious relationship. You wouldn't see them kissing in public, so some people misread that as if it wasn't a romantic relationship, but her boys were often around and the paparazzi were always there, too, so that naturally made them more cautious and less demonstrative to one another. You could still tell that, for him, she was the most important person on the planet.

The inquest lasted for ninety-four days and heard from 278 witnesses. Eventually, after twenty-two hours of deliberation, the jury reached a verdict. They could not agree on a unanimous one, so they handed down a nine-to-two majority verdict of unlawful killing. When it came to allocating blame for the fatal accident, they placed it jointly on Henri Paul and the paparazzi. They decided that Paul was driving too fast and was over the alcohol limit, despite the discredited blood tests, and the paparazzi were blamed for following the vehicle, causing Paul to increase speed then crash into a pillar in the Pont de l'Alma tunnel. The lack of seat belts was cited as a key factor in the resulting deaths.

Afterwards, I felt sorry for Al-Fayed. Some of his wilder theories, about there being a high-level conspiracy to assassinate

Diana and Dodi, were born out of frustration because he wasn't getting answers. He had lost his son but the media had no sympathy for him and they mocked any notion that there may have been anyone other than members of the paparazzi at the scene as little more than a conspiracy theory.

400 KALASHNIKOVS

At more than 13,000 feet, the runway at Berbera airport is the longest in Africa. It's so long that NASA used it as an emergency landing strip for the space shuttle. The rest of the airport is not so special. When I landed there in 2013, it was tiny, loud and full of noisy, aggressive people with weapons and I thought, *Bloody hell, I'm going to be training some of these guys.*

Baggage reclaim was an experience. There was a long line of security police there with big sticks, and they were needed. They were clubbing the locals to keep them back and prevent them from nicking all of our luggage. I just managed to grab my bag before it went. Welcome to Somalia, Lee.

Somalia is one country, which consists of eighteen different regions, at least two of which, Somaliland and Puntland, believe themselves to be independent states. Everyone was taking money from everyone else out there and it was a very chaotic and dangerous country to be in. It seemed like almost everybody was high on khat and you'd see them chewing the leaves all the time. It's imported from Ethiopia and turns up in massive trucks that are loaded with the stuff. Those who chew it experience euphoria and can sometimes become manic. Just what you need in a fairly lawless place where lots of people carry weapons. There had been more than twenty years of violence in Somalia by then, caused by factional fighting, civilian genocide and a civil war. It is often described as a "failed state" and is well known as the base of the infamous Somali pirates. In short, the place was a mess.

I didn't know a lot about this job before I signed up for it but was told I was going to a training camp and the only thing anyone seemed to know about it was that it was shit. There, I would be training police officers to become members of the SFU—a special police unit that would protect Westerners brought in to help stabilize the country and start everything up again. I was working with a company who was operating out of Hereford and they had offered me good money for a training stint in Somalia, so off I went to the Somaliland embassy, which is in a crazy-looking, run-down building in Whitechapel that was full of crap. There were only a couple of Somali guys there but they were nice enough. They took my money, stamped my passport and off I went.

I had a lot of gear to carry with me but I had put my back out again while sparring so I was struggling with it all and was in a lot of pain. Thankfully, I was at least sitting in the comfort of first class on Ethiopian Airlines, which is rare on a job, though I was used to it myself, having worked for Al-Fayed. I flew to Addis Ababa and from there I got my flight to Berbera airport.

While I was waiting to go to the camp, I had a couple of nights in a hotel and it wasn't too bad. The air conditioning even worked, a bit. The place was in a compound right on a beach that had black magnetic sand and huge ghost crabs scuttling along it. You could walk on the beach but you had to be careful. I could see big ships and tankers in the sea and knew there would be pirates out there trying to take them so they could ransom the ships and their crews.

To get to the military training camp, I had to drive out into the desert for two and a half hours. I went with a guy I knew called Paul, who was ex–Special Forces and was also on this job with me. Previously, a group of ex–Royal Marines had been training these police guys but only for an hour or two at a time. But then they and the British embassy protection team were attacked and had to evacuate sharpish. Things had been quiet for a year or more now, so we were sent in to train them properly and not just for short stints every day, but the situation was still pretty chaotic out there. The oil concessions for the area had been sold twice, once by Somalia and then by Somaliland, which didn't help.

The camp was in the middle of nowhere and it was huge. There was a big parade square with a large hole right in the middle of it because the last lot that were in there had dug it up to hide their ammo. I noticed a couple of shot-up "technicals" parked nearby, which wasn't a good sign. That's the nickname for a "non-standard tactical vehicle" (NSTV): a civilian pickup truck or 4x4, with armor plating added and a heavy machine gun mounted on it. You often see vehicles like that in areas of conflict in Africa and the Middle East.

There was a smaller camp within the main camp and we were based inside that. Its walls had barbed wire or broken glass on top. Once inside, we met the two other guys who were already on the job. They were both ex–British Army and unpleasant blokes so I've changed their names to Mike and Dave. They showed us to our room, which was full of ancient wooden rifles and shit that hadn't been touched for years. It was in a small accommodation block, which had become the dumping ground for the camp's rubbish. It was disgusting. There were two metal beds with mattresses and that was all we were given. Thankfully, Paul and I had bought duvets and mosquito nets.

The place where we were about to bed down looked like a factory that hadn't been used for twenty years. There was no glass in the windows and we had to tie brooms to the beds just to put the mozzie nets up. There was one shower and one toilet. All of our water came from a tank on the roof that was filled up by a guy who was supposed to come every seven days but sometimes he didn't. Then we would have no water for a week. We had to get supplies from the "local" town, Hargeisa, the Somaliland capital, which was a ninety-minute drive away. We had no comms either, just a VSAT (very small aperture terminal) system that wasn't working. We had limited power from a generator and, over time, as Mike and Dave pissed him off, the commandant would deliberately switch it off, leaving us with no power at all. There were cockroaches everywhere too. If you went to the toilet in the middle of the night there could be a thousand of them on the floor around you. It wasn't exactly the best environment for a man in his fifties to be working in and this was going to be my home for the next eight weeks. St. Tropez it wasn't, but beggars can't be choosers.

Paul and I both thought the other two guys were a bit funny with us but we got on with it. We were training groups of eighty to a hundred men from the Somali police at a time. If they passed our course, their new skills would see them upgraded to the SPU (special police units) and their wage quadrupled.

Getting through this meant a lot to them as it would have a big impact on their lives.

Dave and Mike had already been in country for a couple of weeks, supposedly getting the course program together. Dave was team leader but Mike told him what to do. They explained, "Each course is split into three: one group is on the shooting range, one does riot control, walking drills and enter and exit, and the third does patrolling, first aid and military drills."

I asked what exactly they wanted us to teach and was told, "You are fucking teachers, aren't you? So, teach."

Nice. And that was on day one.

The next day, training commenced at 6:00 a.m. on the parade square in forty-five-degree Celsius heat. The candidates turned up wearing all sorts of uniforms. Some didn't even have laces in their boots and these guys were the "special police"! A lot of their weapons were useless too. Some were really old or had no sights; others had no stocks. We asked for four hundred new AK-47s but this caused a big argument with the garrison commander. That colonel said his men didn't need new weapons when they clearly did. Basically, he wanted to keep the money for the weapons for himself. He lost his temper big-style and started shouting that his men could already shoot and he threatened to show us how well they could do this by actually attacking us. I remember thinking, *Fuck, he means it!*

Thankfully, he was talked out of launching an assault on us, but he did insist that his men, many of whom were high on khat, follow us all down to the shooting range. When we got there, he said, "I'll fucking show you!" He picked up a weapon and aimed at the target. He sent about twenty rounds down and managed to hit the target with just one. He looked at me then and I was thinking, *Oh shit, he's furious and they are going to kill us all.* Instead, he just smiled at me, threw the gun on the floor and said, "You can have your weapons."

The money was found to pay for four hundred Kalashnikovs but we only received two hundred of them. Coincidentally, the colonel turned up later with his officers and they were all driving brand-new Toyota Land Cruisers.

I was doing riot training with the candidates, and while I was demonstrating a move with an AK-47, this big guy came up and got in front of me. He always wore a white gum shield for some reason and was a well-known and respected man among the guys I was training but he was being a pain in the arse for me that day and trying to undermine me, which I couldn't allow. While I was trying to teach them the move, he told me it wouldn't work and tried to prove his point by grabbing the barrel and the magazine of the gun and wrenching it from my hands, which was dangerous as well as completely disrespectful.

I couldn't allow him to make me look as if I didn't know what I was doing in front of all of these candidates, so I said, "Let's do that again." He was just as keen to show that I was wrong, so he tried to take the weapon from me once more but this time I was playing for real. I had the barrel pointing right at him, and when he went to grab it, I smashed him in the ribs with it and he hit the ground. He was lying on the floor crying, with blood coming out of his mouth and everyone just stared at me.

"Gentlemen," I said, "does anyone else want to have a go?"

No one did. It might sound harsh but in that environment it was the only choice. I had to establish my authority and credibility as an instructor or they would have all stopped listening to me and none of them would have learned anything. He had challenged me and I put the bloke in his place. Not only did I never have any trouble with Gum Shield again but he understood why I had done it and never held it against me. We actually became good friends. It was a bit like the time when my old karate instructor kicked me hard in the throat to set some ground rules and establish respect. We got Gum Shield to the hospital where he was treated for broken ribs and he came back on the course five weeks later, once he had recovered. I shook his hand and told him, "I didn't want to do that and I really want to train you properly, but if people challenge me, I will put them down." He understood and accepted that and we got on great from then on.

Dave and Mike used to speed march the candidates for five miles every day to get them down to the shooting range. But because it was Ramadan, they weren't eating and were collapsing from exertion in the heat and I said they had to stop this but they wouldn't listen to me. We had an ambulance at the camp, but if anyone was in trouble, they didn't use it. I felt that these guys didn't care about the Africans they were training.

The Somalis were not great soldiers, so they often put their fingers on the triggers of their guns instead of keeping them off for safety. Instead of bollocking them for this dangerous act, the other instructors would break their fingers to prove a point. It was awful.

Things got really serious when one of our Somali trainers was bitten by a carpet viper. Soon, the poor guy had blood coming out of his eyes and ears, and before we could get him medical assistance, he tragically died.

That did not seem to soften the attitude of the other instructors, who kept failing the guys on the course. This had a big impact on their lives and cost them a lot of money. By now, the blokes we were training knew that Paul and I were the good guys, but they hated the other two. The situation was getting out of control and becoming very dangerous. Thanks to Mike and Dave, we couldn't even leave the camp anymore. The blokes who had been failed were out there and had put up checkpoints. We heard that they planned to catch and kill us as soon as we left the base. They probably wouldn't have killed Paul and me but we couldn't be 100 percent sure about that. The guys in the garrison had to go out and arrest all of the men who had failed and put them in jail for a while so they could safely let us out.

At the end of every course, there was a graduation ceremony. People from the Ministry of Interior would attend, along with the senior officers, and a band would play. When we reached the last one, everybody was there, including senior guys from the two companies providing the multimillion-dollar contract. The general made a speech and I heard him call out my name and Paul's. The interpreter told me he was saying what a good job we had both done and how grateful he was that we had come to his country to help ensure peace. Everyone clapped.

Then the general turned his attention to Mike and Dave and told everyone what they had been up to. Dave was sitting among us at this point and he could hear everything being said about him because the interpreter was translating it all for him simultaneously. He must have shit himself.

Mike treated these events with complete disdain and wouldn't even attend them. He was standing about four hundred yards away, propped up against a Land Cruiser, looking cocky and not giving a shit, unaware of what was being said about him. Then a hundred eyes turned to stare straight at him and I could see that he was thinking, *What the fuck?*

As soon as the ceremony was over, Paul and I were invited to a banquet, but Dave and Mike didn't go. They were taken straight back to the compound. By the time we returned after the meal, they had their bags packed and were sitting in a vehicle. Hours later, they were gone, on their way out of the country. They had to have an escort out of there or they would have both been killed.

WE ARE GOING TO KILL YOU ALL

With the situation considered more stable in Somalia, the oil exploration companies had started to come back to the country. I went home for a break then came back as a mobile security manager and I started working at this huge area that was still being mapped, swept for mines, cleared and marked with limestone dust.

The company had ten teams doing this, using big bulldozers that were smashing through the terrain in between the chalk lines, marking the area where there was no unexploded ordnance. They had to stay in between those lines, twenty meters apart, to avoid mines.

Behind them came even bigger vehicles with grading machines and spikes to flatten the land, then the seismic machines with vibrating plates followed those, to try to find oil. They were spread out for a mile or two and covered an average of sixteen kilometers a day in forty- or even fifty-degree Celsius and it was often as windy as hell, so you had to wear goggles because you were always being blasted with sand.

There were around thirty blokes on the security team and we were all housed in a four-bedroom villa. It was horrible. You had to get up at 4:30 a.m. to have any chance of getting a shower before you went out on a mission. We were squeezed into the rooms and stacked man to man on cots. Some of the younger guys couldn't hack it. They had done tours of Iraq and Afghanistan that seemed like luxury in comparison. They were often well looked after there, with air conditioning and internet, but here there was nothing. The older guys, like me, who were used to digging in, coped with it better and we tried to look after the younger ones.

I went out to take a look at one of the tented villages the miners used that was in the middle of nowhere. There was a protective fence around it, with about forty guards covering the perimeter and around eighty blokes working from this facility. We went operational to take a look at what was on the ground and I was liaising with everyone but the situation there was very tense and it just got worse and worse. We were attacked by the locals on several occasions and sometimes they actually used spears. It turned out they were furious because the oil exploration company had unknowingly gone right through their sacred grounds.

Then we got a letter from the company, which basically said that the situation had suddenly gone from red, which meant dangerous, to black, meaning it was very serious indeed and anyone who wanted to leave could do it now. This was an unusual scenario and a lot of people were shitting themselves. It felt like we were on a knife edge. That was enough for some of them and they chose to go immediately.

I stayed on and went mobile with my team, which consisted of me, my driver, an interpreter and two more vehicles with eight armed SPU guards. I was mobile operations manager and it was my role to be out there on the ground and moving from site to site to make sure everything was being done properly and safely. It was tense but our local driver cracked me up. He could hardly speak English but somehow he could recite whole lines from episodes of *Only Fools and Horses*, which he loved. When he did it, he even sounded like Del Boy. It was hilarious and a nice way to break the tension.

We parked up on a knoll and that was when "Del Boy," as I always called him, turned serious and said that we should leave. "Mister Lee, I think you should go home." When I asked him why, he told me, "All of the weapons in the area have been bought up. Something is going to happen." This was the kind of local intel you listened to.

Not long after this, we spotted a bunch of de-miners (involved in mine clearance) from South Africa coming down the track. They knew us because they were also employed by the same company and some had been at the overcrowded villa. I was now living in their tented village, too, which we called a fly camp. They gave me a wave as they went by. They were in three teams and they carried on for about three-quarters of a kilometer, until they reached a dry riverbed and there was a contact. They were being shot at and I wanted to get them some support, but the sat phone wasn't working. I couldn't get any signal on my mobile either, but back in HQ they could hear a crackle on their radios and they knew something was happening. I could hear the project manager shouting, "What the fuck is going on?" over the radio. The South Africans didn't hang about. They turned around, bugged out and passed by us at speed. Off they went, so off we went too.

We returned to the same area the next day and were told the local militia were angry and wanted a meeting. I figured I'd better volunteer to represent us but I wasn't looking forward to it. I had to meet these guys in the middle of the desert. Around forty technicals showed up there with loads of people on board. They immediately surrounded us and I was shitting myself. I looked at our special police guys and they all had what I would describe as dead-man's eyes. They were so scared they wouldn't even get out of the vehicle, so they were no help. It was just me and my translator. I got out and stepped into one of the most tense and dangerous situations I had ever been in.

We met their leader and he beckoned for us to crouch down on our haunches, Arab-style, for the meeting. From the beginning, he was angry and he got more and more aggressive as he went on, concluding his opening speech with the words, "We are going to kill you all!" and he definitely looked like he meant it. I didn't know why he was so angry but I had to find out, and quickly, or we would all be dead men.

It took a while but we got to the bottom of it. The company had paid fixers to go out and explain what all the white stuff was on the land because the locals thought they were trying to poison their goats and sheep. The fixers took the company's money but didn't tell anyone what was going on or what the limestone lines were for, leaving the locals worried and angry. Meanwhile, the engineers and their bulldozers were smashing through sacred grounds and really pissing everyone off. I was shocked to hear this and genuinely empathetic with this guy, which helped, and he calmed down a bit. We were down there on our haunches for about forty-five minutes and I managed to get him to come round. I said I would personally ensure that people would come out and speak to him to tell him what was going on. He then decided that he was not going to kill us. At least, not today.

When the meeting was over, he got to his feet to leave but I stayed down there on my haunches, just looking at him. I had decided not to get up until he was gone and I could tell he was a bit uncomfortable with that but, in the end, he left and he took all of his men with him. They drove off in their forty vehicles in a big cloud of dust.

As soon as they were gone, my interpreter, who looked a bit shocked, said, "Lee, I don't know why you did that but it is the bravest thing I have ever seen. You stayed down there and calmly watched him go." He must have thought I was as cool as a cucumber.

I just said, "Mate, I had no choice. I can't move my legs." And I toppled over and landed with a heavy thud in a cloud of dust, then rolled over onto one side. Because we had been down there for so long, my knees had completely seized up but I was determined not to fall over in front of them all or they would have thought I was weak.

I explained to the project manager what had been said at the meeting but he told me the situation was even worse than we thought. The jihadist group Al-Shabaab were pushing into the area now. The intel was that they planned to grab an oil company worker to behead him on live TV. Since we were the only oil and gas company in the region, it had to be us that they were targeting. We got a message from the company to run away and do it fast, so we immediately evacuated the camp.

We managed to get everyone together and everything packed up in just a few hours. It had to be done. The situation was so dangerous that we couldn't guarantee anyone's safety anymore. We figured our only choice was to fly everyone out of there before it was too late.

Eventually, we located a strip of desert that was flat enough to get a light aircraft in to land and pick up the clients but it was a twelve-seater, so we could only put a dozen of them on at a time. Now, these executives and engineers were bricking themselves because they had heard about the plan to behead one of them, so they were screaming and desperate to get away. They were pushing and shoving and fighting each other to get on this plane and that happened every time it returned because they knew that time was running out. Officially, there was a loading list, but when they were due to get into the vehicle to head to the plane, that list went out the window. People were pushing and sometimes punching each other to get on board. It was the effects of adrenaline caused by fear. I even had to drag one guy off the bonnet of the vehicle before it left.

The plan was for the pilot to fly them out to Djibouti, a dozen at a time. The trip there and back took about ninety minutes, and we aimed to do the whole operation in just seventy-two hours. Every time the plane landed, we would put another twelve guys on board then say to the pilot, "See you in an hour and a half."

We finally got the last of the clients onto the plane ready to fly out, leaving only the security team still on the ground. As usual, just before he flew out, we told the pilot, "See you in ninety minutes." But this time he leant out the cockpit window and told us, "I'm not coming back." He then took off and left us standing there stranded in the middle of the desert.

This was a fairly major "oh shit" moment. What were we going to do now?

It seemed our only choice was to try to get back to Berbera over land, to the airport we first flew into, but that was a fair way and there was another problem. We had been tasked to take the big seismic machines out with us. They were very valuable vehicles but would only move at a maximum speed of eleven miles per hour, so it would take us nine hours to get out of there.

I volunteered to go with the seismic machine convoy and told myself that at least we were moving away from Al-Shabaab, while hoping they wouldn't follow us because there was no way we could outrun them.

I was in charge of the rear section of that convoy and there was another guy who took charge of the front. The lads called him "Walter," after the character Walter Mitty, because they thought he had exaggerated claims about his career. That didn't matter too much right now, or it wouldn't have done if he had been able to cope with the stress.

We set off at a painfully slow pace, going over dirt tracks, and we had to stop every couple of hours to let the seismic machines cool down, which was far from ideal when we wanted to get away from danger as fast as possible. The strain of it all got to this bloke and, after a couple of hours, he started behaving erratically. For his own safety I had to take him off that job in the middle of the desert. I told him, "You need to get into that vehicle now because you are done." Then I put him in with a South African lad and said, "Look after him and don't let him out."

Our convoy crawled along for another seven hours but we weren't attacked and finally we got back to Berbera, put the vehicles in the compound then we went to our hotel. We were told the same guy from Djibouti was flying into the airport to collect us, but our relief was short-lived. We discovered the airport was closed and locked down, so we couldn't get in.

I went to see the project manager to see if he could help us but he was scared and stressed out. His team had managed to get hold of a load of booze that had been left behind and all of them were completely wankered. The project manager was stumbling drunk and slurring his words, so it was obvious I wouldn't get any sense out of him. There were twelve of us left in my team, so I got them all together and we set off for the locked-down airport.

Sure enough, there were big chains on the doors and there was no way we could get in to reach our plane. We didn't know what we could do about that but then I looked through a gap in the door and, amazingly, I saw a familiar figure standing there just on the other side of it. It was only bloody Gum Shield, the man I had knocked down and injured on the shooting range.

I banged on the door and he saw me. "Mr Lee!" he shouted, then he got some military people there to unlock the doors for us. We were in!

Gum Shield and I had a little man-hug because we got on really well, despite the fact that I had broken his ribs. It's a good thing he wasn't the type to bear grudges!

Though we were now inside the airport, our problems weren't over because we were stuck there. The military blokes didn't want us to leave, even when we offered them money to ease our way out of there. We managed to bluff and argue our way across the airport and I told Gum Shield, "Do not leave me," as he seemed to be the only one with any influence now. They put us in a holding area and wouldn't let us leave. Worse than that, we could now see our aircraft standing on the runway some way from us. We were desperate to get to it, but if we tried, we knew they might open fire on us. If we just stayed there and waited, the whole place was likely to be overrun by Al-Shabaab, and either way, our plane wouldn't wait for long. The situation was as tense as hell now.

I spotted a combi van outside and I made a decision. "Right, lads, let's go."

We forced the doors open and went straight to the vehicle, climbed inside then got the driver to take us to the plane. We could see that the guys behind us had realized what we were doing and they looked as mad as hell. They were shouting and pointing their guns at us and I was thinking they were going to open up and shoot us but all they hurled at us were insults.

We got out to the aircraft, climbed on board and off we went.

"Freedom, baby!" What a relief.

THE COMPOUND

W hen I left Somalia, I called one of the specialist security companies I knew because I needed a new job fast.

I had lost a lot of money when we had to evacuate before the contract was up. It was one of those jobs that could have gone on forever but now, suddenly, it was done, so I couldn't afford to hang about. I was at the airport when I called them, wearing all of my kit from Somalia and I still had red sand in my boots.

"I've just got back and I need a job," I told them. They were worried I was overqualified but I convinced them I really needed a job and I'd be fine. Within a week they had flown me out to Libya where hundreds of companies were employing thousands of private contractors in a volatile environment.

Out there, I was working with what was known as a "stabilization unit." They were a mixture of British government people and private contractors and their role was to go into places following a conflict and help to stabilize the country. They would train and advise and aim to get contracts for UK companies while the country was getting back to normal.

The British embassy was in Tripoli Towers, on the Al Kurnish Road in the Libyan capital, but we were based in a compound that was between twenty-five minutes to an hour away, though that journey could take two or even three hours on a bad day.

We lived in a villa outside that compound. It wasn't secure but there was at least a checkpoint and it was gated. I had between six and eight bodyguards with me while I was there to guard the clients who came over, and these were pretty important people. During that time, we looked after very senior officials and former high-ranking military officers.

It was fairly safe out there in the immediate aftermath of Colonel Gaddafi's overthrow, following the Arab Spring, but it was always an edgy place. You needed security protocols but we could still drive around the city with local drivers. Being shot at was rare but it did happen, though it was usually not targeted. In those early days, you could still go for a coffee and most people loved the Brits, which was probably a legacy from our presence there during the Second World War. They hated the Yanks though.

The situation changed very quickly toward the end of my six-month contract. We were getting contacts, fighting had started in the city and a police unit we mentored got shot and killed moments after we walked around a corner after chatting to them. I walked a client to a coffee shop and a guy shot another man in the head on the street just a couple of feet from us and casually walked away. I got another client out of a building one day and we almost walked into a massive firefight. I went out to see if it was safe to leave and sheltered behind a dushka (a Soviet-era heavy machine gun) mounted on a 4x4 and picked up a casing ejected from the gun as the militia man let loose on someone. It burned my fingers a little but I still have that casing. The noise was deafening and it felt like the air moved all around you when it was fired. It was pretty scary.

On the ground, when you are doing this kind of work, you have no support. There is just you and your wits. All you can really rely on is your training and resilience. That's it. You are on your own.

Once the role of the stabilization unit was completed, I left. Maybe I should have turned my back on Libya for good since it was so dangerous, but following the collapse of our business, I needed the money from another contract. It also helped me mentally to be away from it all for a while and it was clear that I was needed in Libya.

I could have worked at the British embassy then but I didn't fancy that. There was a massive team there but I thought the rot had set in. People had gone stale and were moaning a lot. A job with a multinational, specialist advisory force seemed like a better bet. They were trying to firm up porous borders in conflicted countries. They would go to ports, border crossings and airports and advise how to stop terrorists getting in. The pay was higher and it looked interesting. It was at first but very quickly the situation around us started to deteriorate.

I was appointed close protection coordinator and organized all of the missions for the six close protection team leaders based in a fortified compound east of Tripoli. This was the wrong side to be on but they couldn't get in anywhere else. All of the suitable places had already been snapped up by the UN. The compound was a converted old colonial hotel. It had massive grounds, with swimming pools and chalets within its walls and a perimeter that was maybe a mile long. The camp had been fortified with walls made from Hesco barriers—large collapsible wire-mesh containers filled with sand—and sangars—temporary fortified positions to protect sentries. We needed them because, right from the off, we knew it wasn't an ideal location. If the shit hit the fan we would be on our own with no help. The international airport was quite far away from us and we knew Al Qaeda were operating in the vicinity.

The close protection setup had been run by an administrator and my job was to bring an operational angle to it. I worked closely under him and we had six teams whose job it was to take the clients where they wanted to go and get them back safely. The night before, I would get the proposed missions, sort them, carry out dynamic risk assessments and decide which ones we would be prepared to do, then put them into mission-critical order and allocate my close protection teams.

I made sure we had everyone's blood groups in case they were wounded; all our call signs were listed and our weapons and mags sorted. We carried specially shortened, easily concealed M7 rifles from Germany, equipped with ACOG telescopic sights with night vision, and Glock 17s, which are famously reliable pistols that can cope with sand and water without jamming. We were monitored on a tracker, so everybody knew where everybody was all the time. We also had extra vehicles in case one was hit. Our medic was a French bloke who we inherited from the previous company. He was a good guy but he had never been in the French military. We let him have a pistol and a mag only, for his own protection or to shoot himself if he had to because you did not want to be taken by Al Qaeda.

I had an ops room with a board that had all of our missions listed on it. They changed all the time. I would have to filter them and make decisions about which ones we had the capability to do on any given day. Some clients might need to go to the admiralty or the airport, so our guys would take them. Someone else might have a meeting planned in the souk, the Arab marketplace, and others might request a run out to the shops to get groceries or supplies.

We always had too many missions and people hated us because we had to say no to quite a few of them as we didn't have enough manpower for them all, particularly the shopping trips. Sometimes I would have to tell someone, "You can't go to the market at 9:00 a.m. because you did that before and you have to vary your routine." That was for a good reason. Routine helps anyone planning an assassination or a kidnapping, so it pays to mix things up.

I had intelligence coming in from lots of different places—from local drivers and fixers and, of course, the British embassy team would unofficially share intel with us. I might get a call from the embassy to tell me there had been a shooting somewhere or someone from NATO just had a contact with insurgents, so we would avoid those places or delay our mission.

It was our job to keep everybody safe and some of the clients seemed to understand that but some did not. I remember there was a famous coffeehouse in Tripoli and a senior official wanted to go there with his staff. I told him he couldn't because it wasn't safe. I had noticed that all of the Westerners were going there, including lots of workers from aid charities. It was a vulnerable place, with naive visitors setting patterns that would be noticed by locals and insurgents. So many Westerners visiting the coffee-house made the place an obvious target so, in my mind, it was out of bounds.

I had to make decisions like this frequently. Clients who knew the score would roll with it, but staff from non-military backgrounds did not always understand the threat. In this instance, we had a disagreement but, at the end of the day, it was my call, so we didn't go. That day, the coffeehouse was shot up and eight people from NATO and one of the other embassies were killed. It was tragic but thankfully we weren't there when it happened because I had identified the threat.

I would insist on knowing where we were going the night before. We had lots of soft-skinned vehicles on the base and I would send a local fixer to do a recce of the location because I wanted to know what was there. Sometimes he would come back and tell me it looked safe and there was no atmosphere. On other occasions, he would say, "Lee, don't go there," because the local militia were doing something and it didn't look safe. Of course, I didn't trust the locals entirely but they knew the score and if they said don't go, then you didn't go.

Some clients thought they were safe when they weren't, not really. I went to one of the ministries and a guy there showed me his office. I was looking for escape routes in case the place was attacked and I couldn't see any. He said, "Don't worry. I'll be fine if anything happens. We've planned for that. I'll just jump out of the office window and the armored vehicle will come round and pick me up." He thought that was a perfectly feasible plan but his office window was on the second floor. I told him if he tried to jump out of it he would probably break his ankles. The second phase of his evac plan wouldn't have worked either because the side street was too narrow for the armored vehicle to get down to pick him up. I made sure he had some rope there, which would at least mean he didn't have to jump all the way. The guy who had agreed to his evac plan was probably a super-fit twenty-eight-year-old Marine, who would have no trouble jumping from the second floor, but this guy was a civilian in his fifties.

Later, we were in his office when some rounds started hitting the building. I took him out the way we had come in. I'm in charge of the client when that kind of thing happens and it was a far more sensible way to get him out of there sharpish than chucking him out the window.

Things started to get more hairy when, very quickly, the situation deteriorated due to the civil war beginning in earnest. The area around us started to get bombarded and the shelling continued day and night. This was not direct fire aimed at us but it was getting closer and the impacts were near enough to make the water in the swimming pool ripple. We were locked down now and the situation got so bad that all of the embassies started to leave. Tripoli airport was too dangerous because it was of great strategic importance and all of the warring factions wanted to take control of it. They say that if you control Tripoli, you control Libya, and if you control the airport you pretty much control Tripoli. A six-week battle began between the Libya Dawn Coalition and the Zintani Brigades, with both trying to seize control of the airport. Twenty aircraft and the airport buildings were destroyed in the fighting.

Everyone who wanted to leave the country now had to use the military airport close to us and most of them came into our compound first, where they would abandon their armored vehicles. Pretty soon, we had a hundred vehicles there. We wanted to get out, too, but that decision was complicated. Locals working for us might be massacred if we pulled out too quickly. It had happened before in another country. It was a legitimate concern, but keeping us in place didn't help us or them and the big worry was that we might be overrun, then all of us would be killed.

The staff were now beginning to panic while desperately trying to find ways out. I drew up a new evac plan because the current one had the civilian advisors driving the armored vehicles themselves while we traveled with them as protection. I pointed out that those guys were not trained to drive armored vehicles. You can't just pick up a set of keys, turn the ignition and go; they have different dynamics to normal cars and you need a high level of tactical driving expertise.

So I started training the staff to drive the vehicles while we were locked down. All the while, you could hear the shelling in the background and there were rockets going over.

I then heard about a new plan that was brewing. There was a French guy who was the head of media. I knew him because, despite being a civilian with no training, he always wanted to carry a gun and he often had a bergen on his back, which looked ridiculous because there was nothing in it. Apparently, this guy wanted to go out and negotiate with Al Qaeda.

I couldn't believe what I was hearing. I was told, "They want your team to do this mission." If anything went wrong, we were supposed to get the French guy out, which was a ridiculous idea. Most likely, we would all be killed.

I heard the details of this crazy plan, stayed as calm as I could then agreed to go to the boardroom and discuss it with the head of mission and the heads of department. This was a big deal. Everyone was panicking about getting out because they realized we could all die here. We went to the meeting and I listened as the French guy laid out the plan, then the head of mission finally asked me my opinion.

I stood up and said, "Sir, it is ludicrous. I refuse to do this because if it goes ahead, everyone will die. It's scandalous that it is even being contemplated."

There was a moment's pause, then the head of mission said, "Thanks, Lee. That's the most sensible thing I've heard all day."

So that brought an abrupt end to the insane plan to send our media guy out to negotiate with Al Qaeda.

YOU HAVE TO SHOOT ME

There were around twenty Brits, a few French and Eastern European guys and ten Jordanian ex-policemen on the security detail, with approximately thirty civilian staff in the camp. By this stage, the cleaners and cooks, who were all locals, had left. Our drivers were getting twitchy and had started not coming in. The Americans had all gone and basically everyone was leaving Tripoli apart from us. We were now starting to take direct fire into the compound from small arms and it was getting really nasty.

Once it became clear that we needed to get out of the country quickly, we had to come up with a plan. It was decided we would go out to the naval base to try to charter or even buy a boat to get us all out of there. I went out with two clients that day, to try to pull off this deal. One was a naval expert and the other knew all about aircraft. If we couldn't get a boat, our backup plan was to try to reach the airport somehow and do a deal to fly us all out. As we left the camp, we knew there was a hell of a lot resting on this.

I sent Graham, my second in command, out first and it was fucking mayhem, with rockets flying by at head height. I reckoned everyone was thinking that if we followed him we'd all die. We waited until it quietened down for a moment and then went for it. We had no choice because we were virtually the last Westerners holding out here now and we would all be killed if we didn't risk it.

It was chaos, with cars whizzing around and blokes with RPGs (rocket-propelled grenades) on their shoulders; there were roadblocks and, as we went by the filling station, there was a live firefight going on between rival militias who were trying to get the petrol, which was in very short supply.

Somehow, amidst all of this chaos we managed to get to the naval area without being killed. It was surrounded by blocks of flats and we had to meet two people there who were supposed to be getting us a boat. The place was an absolute shithole, the building next door had already been rocketed to fuck and there were bullet marks all over the walls. When we went inside, we found two guys there with stacks of money everywhere and our expert started bargaining with them for this boat that they said they could get us.

Pretty quickly, the truth became clear to me. There was no boat but they really wanted our money and we were being set up to be killed. I made a decision then and pretty much dragged our guy from there, while our boys covered us and we got the hell out.

Now we had to get to the airport instead and the next part of the journey was even more chaotic. We were doing all of our counter-surveillance drills, the radios were going nonstop and people were shouting "Left, clear!" "Right, clear!" and "RPGs ahead!" Everyone was super-tense and hyped up; it was fifty degree Celsius and we were all wet through with sweat.

Somehow, we managed to reach the airport, but we had to go down a side road to get into it. It had been a beautiful international airport but now it was a mess. We got stopped at a checkpoint in the middle of what felt like nowhere because it had all been bombed. The meeting was to take place on the first floor of a dilapidated old building. We parked up and I talked to our local driver, who told me we couldn't stop here but wouldn't tell me why, even though I kept asking. Graham went in with the interpreter to speak to the militia about the meeting. They said it's all cool and we decided to go in.

There were the two clients, Graham and me, plus the interpreter. It wasn't the naval guy's area of expertise but I didn't want to leave him in the car because vehicles are basically bullet magnets so, if you don't need to be in them, you get out. We always try to get the clients out of cars if we can. Our armored vehicles, B6 Toyota Land Cruisers, could take small arms fire and very often did, but a direct hit with an RPG would be a different matter.

Before we went in, I made a decision that saved all of our lives. I took the keys off the drivers. I guessed that as soon as we were in the building they were going to drive off. It turned out to be the right call because the guys at the airport were from a different militia and our drivers were convinced they were about to be killed, so they were planning to fuck off and leave us there.

We were in that meeting for maybe ninety minutes, in fifty-degree Celsius heat with no wind or air conditioning and we were drenched in sweat. It was so hot that if you looked at the pavement it would burn your face. The Sahara wind was like having a hot hairdryer constantly pointed at you and we had all our gear on too. We were wearing proper shirts and trousers to look smart, to give us an air of authority.

The meeting seemed to be going okay for a while but then all of a sudden something happened and the militia guys started to get very twitchy and I didn't like it. *That's it,* I decided, *this meeting is finished.* I almost dragged the clients out of there because I knew something was wrong but we were in an entirely militia-controlled area, so we couldn't wave our weapons around or they would open up on us.

We were just getting into our vehicles when it started to go crazy around us, with rockets going over and landing nearby and everything was exploding. It turned out that another militia was coming to try to take the airport so they could control the city. There was ordnance everywhere and we had to somehow get out of there and back to the compound—but to do that we had to go through the advancing militia. They would see our diplomatic plates but they would be surprised to see us because they thought everyone had left by now. Also, they might not give a shit who we were and could open up on us anyway.

Tanks and rocket launchers were letting rip now and we were swerving and dodging. It was absolute mayhem. The clients were shitting themselves and shaking like crazy as we were tearing through the place, and who could blame them?

We were switched on now, in full security mode, or, as we called it, at "Condition Red." The Cooper Color Code is named after the US Army colonel who devised it during the Vietnam War. "Green" is safe and you can switch off; "orange" is "awareness" and a close protection operator is on "orange" all the time; "red" means an attack is about to happen; and "black" is the actual attack.

A lot of people don't understand that you can't effectively go from green straight to black. The adrenaline dump is so high it can make people do bad or irrational things when they are being attacked. You cannot be effective until you get your adrenaline under control. Your fine motor skills won't work until then. If we were going back to the base in a hostile country like Libya and we had a contact, we would radio forward and tell everyone to "Go red!" They would then ready themselves for our arrival at the base.

On a previous mission, one of our vehicles had been contacted and chased for about six kilometers under constant fire. They had to radio ahead so that, as they came in, all the close protection lads were ready outside the compound with weapons aimed so they could engage. That show of strength was enough to see off their pursuers who turned away but the vehicle was shot to hell.

That day we managed to get back from the airport without casualties, which was some kind of miracle. Our compound was now almost the only Western asset between the warring militias and the terrorists and slap-bang in the middle of the opposing factions: General Haftar, ISIS and Al Qaeda to the east and the government forces to the west, holding Tripoli. There was small arms fire and rockets going over the camp. We were trapped inside there now, with no boat or plane to get us home, and we badly needed a new evacuation plan because things were getting desperate. We were not sure now if there even was a way out.

We decided we were going to try to reach the border with Tunisia. We knew it might not be possible but we would all die if we stayed here. No one was coming to rescue us. It was an international mission, which meant that no single country's government was looking out for its citizens.

First we had to take up defensive positions. I was up on the roof. If you have ever seen that Hollywood film *13 Hours: The Secret Soldiers of Benghazi*, it was almost exactly like that, meaning it was incredibly dangerous. At this crucial point, we knew we might have to make a final stand against an attack, so we went to get more ammo. What we were carrying was nowhere near enough. But when we went to break out some more, there wasn't any. All we could find were loads of torches and extendable batons, which were of absolutely no use to us. There were boxes and boxes of shit that you would never use in a battle but no bloody ammo. With no ammunition, we knew we were screwed.

All we could give the Jordanians with us was a single magazine each, and between us all what we had would only have lasted for a short time before we ran out of ammunition completely. We all reckoned we were done. There was no chance at all of holding this position if the compound was attacked. It would have been hard enough with unlimited ammo, but we'd got next to none at this point. The truth began to sink in. It was over.

All that was left for us to do now was to have *that* discussion. The one that involves deciding who is going to shoot who because we would rather die at our own hands than be taken alive by Al Qaeda.

Once it began, it pretty quickly became a quite bizarrely matter-of-fact conversation.

"Right, Graham," I said, "you shoot me, mate."

Then Graham said, "Ritchie, you've got to fucking shoot me then."

Then Jonah chipped in, "Hey, hang on. I'm not going to be the last one, so one of you has to shoot me first. Who's it going to be?"

So we were now having an argument about who was going to shoot who and who would be left at the end because the last one would have to shoot themselves. There was even some banter and very dark humor about it all, but deep down, we were deadly serious. We knew we were going to have to do this.

RUNNING ON FUMES

Just as we had begun to think it was all over for everyone, there was a sudden lull in the battle going on around us while the combatants took a break for prayers. We came back down for a big impromptu meeting with all of the security team, while all around us there was chaos, with people crying and thinking they were going to die. I turned to the lads and said, "Right, this is the score. We are all in the shit but all of us are fucking amazing. Every man here is a professional that I would trust with my life, so we are taking control of this situation right now. We are going to run this evac plan again and we are going to manage it."

And that's what we did. We ran the evac plan again, the way we wanted to do it, and it worked.

That lull in the fighting gave us time to try and find another route out of there, so the mission decided to get a few members of staff out of the country to test the route. We planned everything to the smallest detail and I was tasked to lead a team of six out, including staff who were meant to have already been shipped out on leave. I got hold of a local fixer and two of our Jordanian police lads and we set off with them leading the way up ahead of us, along a pre-planned escape route to the border, to see if it was viable. The fixer had been speaking to the local militia leaders and offered to pay them to escort everyone through, but at this point there was no guarantee of that. There were checkpoints all along the way to the border manned by different groups of militia, while everyone was very aware that Al Qaeda were coming. ISIS were out there, too, somewhere and they all wanted a piece of Tripoli.

We pulled out of the base in a convoy of three armored vehicles. There were burnt-out cars everywhere and people knelt down in the middle of road, pointing RPGs at everyone who passed, including us.

The idea was that every time we were stopped at a checkpoint, our fixer would negotiate our way through with a hefty bribe. The checkpoints were heavily manned by militia in "technicals"— those converted armored vehicles with heavy machine guns. At one checkpoint, I counted ten technicals behind us and ten in front, all armed to the teeth. We were totally outgunned and at the mercy of these militia each time we were stopped, shitting ourselves in case we couldn't get through. We had to sit in our vehicles worrying that if they wouldn't take our money or honor whatever deal had been done, we were fucked.

There is nothing you can do when you are outgunned like that. I heard of one situation where elite Navy SEALs protecting the CIA guys were stopped and everything was taken from them. Thankfully, they let the men go but they lost all of their kit and there was nothing they could do about it.

The money offered at checkpoints was not my responsibility, so I didn't get to hear the exact amounts handed over and it varied but it was quite a lot of cash, in US dollars. We watched the furious haggling going on until, eventually, there were smiles when a price for our safety had been agreed. Those negotiations were high stakes, involving life or death for us all.

We probably went through three or four different gangs of militia manning ten checkpoints. We just had to hope we didn't run out of money and trust that it would work or we would all be dead. We couldn't even shoot our way out if things went wrong. You can't use small arms fire against armed vehicles. Best-case scenario, we would have to leave the vehicles to run away and hide in the desert.

The route should have taken two and a half hours, but it took us nearly five. Luckily, this time we were not shot at along the way and our fixer managed to get us through every checkpoint, though each one was very tense.

When we reached the border, we found tens of thousands of refugees had gathered there on the Libyan side and people had started to panic and were trying to force their way across. When that first happened, the Tunisians on the other side had responded by opening fire and they shot a lot of people. The refugees were still stuck there and the situation was very tense.

We let two Irish nationals leave our party and we watched them go into no-man's-land between the Libyan and Tunisian borders, hoping they would make it across. It was a huge relief when they were finally allowed into Tunisia.

We now knew we could go across that border. Graham, my second in command, and I looked at each other and I said, "I know we can go now if we want to but I'm going back." It would have been so tempting to leave the country and never look back, but we had to return to the compound for everyone else. It wasn't a question of losing my job because that was obviously going to end soon anyway. I just couldn't leave them all behind.

Back we went, retracing our steps, with the fixer going out ahead to the checkpoints and us shitting ourselves every single time we were stopped, until we eventually made it back to the compound. We took everyone out five or ten at a time, each team taking the same route as the one we had rehearsed, while we hoped we could still get through.

The evac plan worked and, once we got all thirty of the staff out, there was only the security team left in the compound and I was finally free to leave. I made a video for my wife and in it I said, "Kate, I am going to try and get out now and I am sure we will make it . . ." but I made sure to say goodbye to her as well, just in case.

The very last members of the British embassy staff were leaving, too, so my plan was to join up with them with three of my lads. We managed to get across Tripoli, reach the British embassy just in time and join the convoy, which had armed contractors who I knew guarding it at the front and the back. We took the same route as before, though mindful that a previous convoy had been shot up along the way. Somehow, we managed to limp toward the border. There were eighteen vehicles in total, all armored, and some of them broke down and had to be left en route.

You can imagine how tense it was at the border crossing point after the Tunisians had opened fire on the refugees. It felt as if anything could happen there.

By now, there was no fuel left in the vehicles and we were running on fumes, praying we would make it across the border before the armored vehicles just ground to a halt. We had made it to the Libyan side of the border and they let us through, but there was still the strip of no-man's-land between that border and the Tunisian side, which we were now stuck in, while the border guards decided whether to let us through or not. We had to shut off the engines before the fuel ran out completely and that meant sheltering under a bridge, sitting in vehicles in fifty-degree Celsius heat with no air conditioning for a couple of very tense hours. During that time, nothing happened and we were stuck in limbo between two countries, with no fuel left for a journey back if we were refused entry.

After what seemed like an eternity, they opened the border and let us through into Tunisia. We were finally out of Libya, leaving a war zone with crazed militias and fanatical jihadists behind us. We were safe at last. The relief for us all was indescribable. You know those clips you see on TV when the pope arrives somewhere and he gets down on his hands and knees and kisses the ground? That was exactly how I felt!

Once we'd refueled our vehicles, I went straight to the hotel I'd pre-booked in Tunis and called Kate. She had gone round to a friend's house to visit, and when my call came in, she had to hang out of an upstairs window to get a signal. I managed to get through to her there and I just said, "I made it."

I had a very long shower then went for a beer and got absolutely pissed. Who could blame me? It wasn't that long since I had been working out which of us would have to shoot the others to avoid being captured by Al Qaeda. But somehow we had made it out of there in one piece.

After barely getting out of Somalia and almost being killed in Libya, I told myself that never again would I go somewhere that bloody dangerous. It was still okay to go abroad and use my skills to train people but I decided it might be a sensible thing to avoid war zones from now on.

IN HARM'S WAY

I had absolutely no intention of ever visiting Libya again. But, around eighteen months after our desperate departure from the country, I got a phone call from a friend I had worked with before. He told me the situation had changed a great deal in the intervening months. Things were much calmer and more secure in Libya and it was no longer a war zone. They were sending people back there to reestablish a compound and a lot of my mates were going. He assured me the war was dying down, and from what I had heard, it looked to me as if it was, so I figured why not?

He asked if I could come out for eight weeks to help to secure and hold a compound. The money was good. I could earn around £7,000 a month tax-free, and although I didn't need the cash at that point, I did need the excitement. Deep down, I knew it would probably be a bit tasty but I had no idea just how bad it would get.

I flew into Mitiga airport in October 2016. The military airbase was the only airport still open at this point. An ex-military mate was there to meet me with his guys and they had four armored vehicles with them, so I assumed they must be picking up a bunch of people.

I asked him, "Who else is coming?"

"No one."

"Then why do you need four armored vehicles just for me?"

"Mate," he said, "the situation has changed."

It was then that the penny dropped. Libya might have been a safe-ish place when I was offered the job, but by the time I'd flown out there, things had gone massively and very rapidly downhill. The militias had calmed down previously but now General Haftar's Libyan National Army was pushing in on Tripoli from the east. He had stopped his forces outside the city and there was a standoff. Everyone was getting ready to fight the final battle.

I couldn't believe how bad things had become in such a short space of time and started to wonder if I was jinxed. To give you a sense of how serious it was, I arrived at the site to find private military contractors, who had been sent in to secure it and make the place safe for staff to move back in, now walking round openly talking about dying.

From the outset, we were on the streets getting as much intelligence as we could on the situation. I was the first Westerner to walk back into the American embassy compound that was smashed up after it had been abandoned in 2014 and I got to see what happens when the militias break in. The place was an absolute mess. There were bullet holes in all of the walls and blast damage to the buildings. Inside, every room had been trashed. I could feel the anger of the people who had done this and did not fancy being on the receiving end of it in our compound.

Things were as bad as we first thought and they were about to come to a head. There was going to be a big battle and we were trapped right in the middle of it. We knew we were on our own. It was big boys' rules from now on. We put up firing points and got together as much weaponry and ammo as we could find. Luckily, this time there was enough for us to at least make a stand. We had enough ammo for fifty guys and there were twelve of us, all armed to the teeth.

We had to carry our protective equipment, kit and ammo around with us at all times because we knew an attack could happen at any moment. We worked out protocols to use if the insurgents came at us over the wire. We each had our firing positions and would use them to fight back toward the roof, which would be the place to make our final stand. We christened it "the Alamo," and with good reason.

I was standing in the ops room at the compound when an admin guy came to see me. He told me he had been tasked with getting everyone to comply with the ISO (International Organization for Standardization) standards. Around us, there was absolute chaos and all hell breaking loose. We were fixing thick metal plates to walls to make firing points, putting sandbags in strategic positions to prevent the compound being overrun and parking vehicles so they blocked entryways. While we were in the middle of doing all this, the bloke said, "Just a quick one. I am going to need all of your men to bring their laptops and mobile chargers in for me to check them." Somehow, he hadn't grasped that we were in a war zone and the situation around us was deteriorating rapidly. He wanted to check that all of our equipment met an international standard when what we cared most about at that point was staying alive.

I deflated him a little bit by pointing out that worrying about ISO right now was a pointless load of absolute bollocks, then I told him to fuck off out of my sight and sent him on his way.

We didn't even have an evac plan this time because the situation was too dangerous and chaotic for that, but we did need a way out of the compound if we were attacked and the front gates were breached by insurgents. A part of the wall had been built as a single skin, so we reckoned you could bust through it with an armored vehicle if need be. That became the plan. We would pile into the armored vehicles and the first one would drive straight at the wall and hopefully get through it. The others would go after it and exit through the new gap in the wall. That's how desperate we were.

After that, it was going to be every man for himself and we'd have to split up then hit the road. We knew we wouldn't get very far in a large group with the armored vehicles, so we started to form smaller groups, each with a different plan for escape. I was seriously contemplating flagging down a car, hijacking it at gunpoint and getting it out of the city, so I could drive through the desert to the border if I had to. Others figured they would steal a boat. It was desperate stuff.

At this point, I didn't just feel frightened and worried; I also felt really bad because I was putting my family through all of this again and it was my fault. This was the third time I had found myself in a war zone, with limited control over what would happen to me. I had to ask myself, *What is compelling me to keep putting myself in danger like this?* I don't think I really came up with a good answer. There had to be an easier way to make a living but I had yet to find it.

I had to admit that, after finding myself in situations as scary as the ones in Somalia and the last time I was in Libya, strange as it may sound to normal people, you can find that you do miss that level of excitement. Normal life can feel a bit mundane by comparison and you miss the challenges jobs like this provide.

That did not mean that I had a death wish or I didn't care what happened to me; I was very keen to get home and live happily ever after with my wife and family. I was no longer a young and reckless man. At fifty-four years of age, I should really have known better. Once again, I told myself, *After this one, Lee, no more war zones.* In the future, I would happily train men in countries like Nigeria and Saudi Arabia, but my days of going into areas of conflict were definitely over now. Of course, I still had to get out of this bloody mess first.

We calculated we had enough ammo to put up a good fight but that it would probably last for only a short time before we were overrun. We had limited medical supplies, so if anyone was shot they would probably bleed out and die from their wounds. The consensus was that we were fucked.

For four weeks we were stuck like this, seeing little chance of getting out of there alive and just waiting for the final attack that would finish us off. In the end, our salvation came from the most unlikely of sources. We were saved by ISIS.

Until those militant Islamists started to turn up in numbers, the various militia groups were at each other's throats and ready to go to war with one another. All of a sudden, they had a common enemy because none of them wished to see their country fall to extremists who wanted to plunge Libya back into a dark-ages caliphate. The warring sides started talking then at a high level about the best way to unify and stop the ISIS fighters. As a result, things gradually began to calm down.

After a few weeks, the situation had improved to the point where I could drive down to Mitiga airport, where a fixer had prearranged safe passage out of the country for me and my medic-driver, John. He had to do this because the airport was now under the control of a militia that had sympathies leaning toward Al Qaeda, which made them very dangerous people to do business with. I was hoping for a quiet evac out of there, but as I walked through the airport, I didn't exactly blend in. Being the only white guys there, we stood out a mile and were soon intercepted. All of our kit was taken from us. We were put into a room and held there by armed militia. The fixer did his bit to explain things and the militia took our passports then left us there under armed guard. I sat in that room for three hours wondering what would happen next. Would they let me go or shoot me? Finally, we were ushered out of the room and put on a plane, sharpish.

When you are on a plane in a place like that and it rises into the air with its wheels up, it is a wonderful feeling. It feels even better when that plane gets out of RPG range.

THE PRICE OF FAME

I had made the transition from being a close protection body-guard for hire to the man you could come to today for every aspect of your personal security for you, your home and your family. With all of my experience and contacts in the industry, I am often approached by big companies to take a consultancy role with them. I usually work with people I know well but I also set up my own company, The Operator's Circle, to help with the vital task of identifying the right people for each job. So how would we pick the right person to protect you?

When we advertise a job we might get two thousand applicants, but probably 80 percent of those candidates will be unsuitable for one reason or another. Once we have interviewed a shortlist of twenty or so people, we then do a background check on each of them. Here, contacts really do matter. If the candidate is ex-military, I might know their old RSM (regimental sergeant major). If they have already done a job, at the Australian embassy in Kabul, say, there is a very strong chance I will know their project manager. If they are new to the business, I will speak to the guy who taught them on their close protection course. If any of those people have a negative opinion of a candidate then it's a "no" from us and we don't consider taking them.

Close protection jobs are split into tiers. A tier three job might involve meeting a VIP or celebrity who is coming to London and wants a bodyguard to accompany them on a night out. Tier two could be working abroad at an oil or gas site or protecting a foreign embassy. Tier one requires the very best people to look after vulnerable, high-net-worth individuals for an extended period of time.

A lot of people want to be rich or famous and they probably don't consider the downside to that. If you are genuinely famous, to the point where everybody instantly knows who you are, that can make you a target. If you are rich, you can be sure there is someone out there who would like to take your money away from you by any means possible, using violence if necessary. People who are born rich or who have gradually become very successful tend to understand that they will need security, but what about those rare individuals who become rich and famous overnight? What about the singer whose debut album suddenly goes platinum or the actor who has a breakout movie and becomes the hottest thing in Hollywood? They might be in for a rude awakening because they don't yet know the dangers they will face. That's where I come in.

How I react to a request for security depends on the nature of the threat. Sometimes, it is a slow burner, as the client has grown into their situation and the security team has to grow with them. They may be a businessperson who has chosen in advance to become involved in a high-risk venture because the rewards outweigh the security risks and they need a pre-planned response, which is always better. That gives us the time to plan ahead and the ability to think, *What if this were to happen?*

Occasionally, though, it can be a high-risk, dynamic request because something unexpected has suddenly occurred and the threat to the principal has quickly gone from zero to massive. They need protection and they need it now. Most likely they have no idea what they require to keep them safe. That's when they put in a call to me.

Some clients want a single IBG (individual bodyguard) while others end up needing a sizable team that could be anything from a handful of people to a hundred members, if the principal is a seriously high-risk individual. A single bodyguard has a very tough role as they have to do everything on their own and that is the most difficult job in the industry. You might be hired for one occasion, to take someone to a red carpet event, for example, and that is easier, but protecting someone for an extended period of time on your own is hard and one person will not be sufficient to ensure the safety of some clients.

The location of the client and their security team matters too. In a lot of countries, you are allowed to carry weapons, but not in the UK. If they are UK-based, their people cannot be armed, which is a whole new ball game.

Everyone's circumstances are different, but I'll give you a hypothetical situation to show the security I offer to keep people safe. Some of it might seem obvious but a lot of it is specialist stuff you might never have thought of. Let's say that we have a couple who have suddenly become very wealthy and extremely famous but it has happened so quickly that security is something they hadn't really thought about before. He is a Premier League footballer who has recently made a big breakthrough and become an international name; she is a pop singer with a year's worth of hits and they have suddenly turned into the Posh and Becks of their generation.

Now, let's throw in a massive threat to them. Let's say they were carjacked on their way home and robbed by violent criminals. She's been stuffed in the boot of the car and he is tied up on the back seat, while a gang robs them of everything: watches, jewelry, electronic devices then finally their luxury car. They saw the people who did this and they are members of one of the biggest criminal gangs in the UK, so the threat to them now is massive. They don't know what to do. They don't even know what to say to the police because they have been told that if they talk to them, they will be killed.

That would be a shocking situation for anyone to be involved in and a huge wake-up call for our newly famous couple. Their old lives are over. They would need protection immediately to prevent something like this from ever happening again. That's when men like me step in and provide security so they don't have to spend the rest of their lives in fear.

The first thing I would do is get them away from there. I would want them out of their current home until we had fully evaluated it and carried out work there, assuming they wanted to stay in the house. We would turn it into a place where they could sleep easy in their beds at night without constantly worrying about a break-in. We would spirit them away to some remote location for a while, perhaps in Wales or Scotland, and make sure no one but us knew where they were. I would have guys living in with them at that stage. They would more than likely want that, at least to begin with, following the shock of the robbery. The close presence of bodyguards twenty-four hours a day would be reassuring.

At the new place, we would have escape routes worked out, including spots identified for helicopter landing, in case we had to bug out of there quickly. We might have a dog with us when we patrol the area. We would use local, hired cars and turn up with everything we need as portable kit. That would include alarms, cameras, night vision, medical kits, trauma packs and our comms and we would set up all of it in this residence. We would keep the couple there while we hardened the security in their home, so work would be going on in their house while they were away.

Let's assume they have a lot of money and are not frightened to spend a sizable chunk of it to ensure their safety. It might take a million or possibly even two million pounds a year to give them everything they need, as none of this is cheap. I would go in and do a security risk analysis for the client then detail all of the measures needed to protect them, including the manpower required and the physical items we would have to put in for them. Cost is always an issue but is offset against the risk to their safety. They also have to consider the compromise to their lifestyle and the effect on their relationship from having all this security around them. If they perceive the risk as being really high, they will usually come up with the cash required to have security at the level I would recommend.

My job is to sit down with them and explain to the whole family and all of the workers at the house or the estate what the risk is and what they have to do to stay safe. We have to take the insurance companies into consideration too. People who are valued over a certain amount of cash, running into the millions, are required to have certain security measures in place in order to get insurance. That could mean teams of two or three people there at all times, as a minimum requirement.

A couple might not always agree on the level of security they need, particularly if one of them stays home and the other goes out a lot and experiences a greater risk. The one who stays at home might say, "It's too expensive." Or, "I am not having a camera there or a security fence here or people in my garden." So we might end up giving them a version of what we want, what he wants and what she wants, so it becomes a complicated matrix. As the risk to them goes up, so does the likelihood of them reaching an agreement on a full package of measures. If their kid goes to school without security and that child suddenly gets approached by someone, then it is another escalation of threat and the kind of incident that makes them agree between them to pay whatever it costs.

The object of the exercise is to keep these people safe for their own sakes but it would also impact on my professional reputation if I failed to do that, so I want to make sure they have everything they need.

We would start with the RST (residential security team). They will be in charge of looking after the couple's residence or residences. They will lock it down at night and make sure everything is checked and double-checked throughout the day. They will install CCTV and ensure there is enough lighting to illuminate every dark corner, so no one slips by. The perimeter will be protected with detection monitors and alarm systems and, ideally, patrolled with dogs.

There would be electronic anti-surveillance and counter-surveillance measures and at night they would sweep the place for bugs. They also sift, check and X-ray every item of incoming mail. Everyone would be booked in and out, so they would know who was in the residence at all times. They would have medical equipment in case it was needed and if the couple travel by heli-copter, they would manage the ground-to-air communications with the chopper. Crucially, they would be in charge of the safe room, making sure that everything in there was in date. That would include all of the supplies and water, and they would check that the air ventilation system and the comms were all working. A safe room will have steel-reinforced doors and walls as well as bullet-resistant panels. Once you are inside, no one is getting in.

There would probably be other tasks that are particular to the client. We had to lock the chickens up at night for one of ours then let them out again in the morning. That might sound a bit trivial but it prevents the principal from having to leave the house to do it themselves and makes them less vulnerable. The duties of the team could include anything that helps the client. The RST will even get a brew on in the morning for the close protection team when they come in to take over and escort the principal when they leave the residence. Ideally, they would have their own living accommodation and an ops room on site, preferably removed from the rest of the house in order to keep a lower profile and stay out of the family's way, but that is not always possible.

The close protection team will consist of a team leader, a PPO (personal protection officer) who is a bodyguard and PES (personal escort security) to create a further ring of security to take out the threat before it gets near, while the bodyguard gets the principal out of harm's way. Sometimes, ego dictates that the team leader is also the bodyguard, but ideally you don't want that. It is best if the team leader is away from the client, so they can concentrate on leading the team.

When the principal leaves the residence, the close protection team stays with them and returns them to the RST at the end of the day. They might have duties in the residence but they often work long hours, so generally they take them out and bring them back and that's it. The close protection team are there to mitigate the threat, so the principal can get on with their normal life without worrying about anything, albeit with all of this security around them.

All forms of attack would be taken into account, not just physical. That includes cyber or bugging and even photographic, from the media or other parties, which can be embarrassing for the principal. We will do counter- and anti-surveillance to deny any person who is paid to attack the principal, whether that is a physical assault or through business, by damaging their image, or from opportunistic attacks, such as road rage. Sometimes the threat can come from mentally impaired people, such as stalker-fans, which are a big issue for a lot of celebrities. We will also mitigate risks from possible accidents, such as their kids playing somewhere dangerous or their wives riding a horse without a protective hat. We are also responsible for all of their stuff and that includes their phones, laptops and any other electronic devices. If they got pissed in a bar and accidentally left their phone behind, we would spot this and pick it up for them.

At the residence, we would have layers of security, starting with the outside perimeter. This should now be a fence, with cameras and sensors, so that anyone who goes near it or touches it would set off an alarm. That would be the first warning that someone was trying to get in, and the RST would spot them on camera.

Next, we would have inner circles of defense. The second layer could be physical, a smaller fence perhaps, as well as other obstacles, such as electronic wires or beams that they have to pass. There will always be several levels of warning in case one of them fails. We will ask ourselves, "What happens if that layer fails?" so we always have a fallback position.

By now, everyone will know there is an intruder and they are stood to. The RST go into their "actions-on," enacting the response we have planned in advance. The close protection team will be woken up and they will stand to as well. Everyone has their positions and knows their role. It could be that the close protection team deploys inside the house while someone else gets the cars ready for an evac, or we might get the principal to the safe room and keep them there until the police come.

Hard security measures might involve putting in blast-glass and steel doors with reinforced doorframes that can't be kicked in. A safe room can be bought and installed or you can make one from what they have already got there. We'd have personal panic alarms with transmitters and fire ladders leading to escape routes. A professional company would come in and install all of this for us, using the latest technology. We will have a geofence that uses technology to set up a virtual perimeter and triggers an alarm if a person or electronic device enters it. We will know anything that is going on inside that area because anybody who steps inside will be flagged up.

The RST team might consist of two, three or four people whose job it is to secure the premises, working days and nights. They might not necessarily be tier-one or tier-two bodyguards, though. They could be new or inexperienced, perhaps even on their first gig, or they could be experienced operators who just prefer this level of work. They will have all done the SIA (Security Industry Authority) course in close protection. That's a two-week course that tells you the basics.

The Royal Military Police, the police and 22 SAS all do their own close protection courses, and people from any of these backgrounds can do the conversion course to get the badge they need to work in the UK on most private jobs. The majority of operators who have taken the police and military courses are really good but they are used to doing it with weapons. It's a game changer in close protection when you have no weapons.

Generally, I work with former military and some ex-police, as well as some civilians, though they haven't usually been in hostile environments, and nor have the police, apart from in Northern Ireland, perhaps.

The course teaches you loads of stuff, including protocols in close protection, threat and risk assessment, security and personal awareness, surveillance—including counter- and anti-surveillance—IED searches, general searches and operational planning. You are taught how to do venue and route recces, which are more likely to be used in hostile situations. You learn to choose an A-route, a B-route and a C-route in case you are compromised and need a backup plan.

Venue recces can be done in depth in advance or they can be a dynamic one that you do quickly on arrival. What's in the building? Where are the escape routes? How do you get out of there fast if you need to? What are the fire protocols and where do you sit? Where would be safest if there is a blast? If you think you could be attacked, who sits where? Who is on the guest list, where do the cars go, where do you drop off and pick up? Are there local factors that might affect things, like when the nightclub kicks out? After all that evaluation, do you even go there or pick another place instead?

On the courses I run, we live together for two weeks and we are out all the time on exercises. We tell people where to walk, how to get through a crowd, how far away you should be from the principal—everything. There are driving drills on some courses, but surprisingly it is not actually a requirement. You receive some basic medical training, including how best to respond when you are the first person on the scene. If you continue to take courses in close protection, that medical knowledge and training could eventually go right up to almost paramedic level.

The SIA course is inadequate but it is a compromise with cost and time. Even that course could take four weeks and set you back as much as £4,000, for training that will get you into the industry but you still might not get a job. The course does not reach the standard the industry wants but it does reach the standard the government requires. The bulk of your knowledge will come from professional courses later and, as in most careers, you learn the skills on the job. It's like passing your driving test and only then learning how to actually drive.

There is no requirement to learn close-quarter combat skills, which might surprise people, but no one can agree on a national standard for it. On my courses, we do a lot of close-quarter contact training because that is my bag, so I do the training myself.

You might be wondering how we can possibly protect a high-risk principal without weapons when those who wish to do them harm might have no worries about breaking the law and could choose to carry guns. It's incredibly important to make your location hard enough to get into because then some people are not even going to try. Their surveillance will reveal some of the measures you have put in place and at that point they will probably choose to walk away. For criminals, there always has to be a payoff, so if they can get into your property, commit a profitable crime and leave safely afterwards then that is what they will do, but they prefer to pick the lower-hanging fruit. In an area with a lot of high-net-worth individuals, we know the likelihood of homes being broken into is quite high. We just have to make sure that the victim is not us. The measures that we put in place will make most people go and seek an easier target elsewhere.

There is nearly always surveillance before any kind of attack. It could be a short surveillance or it could go on for years. We will do whatever we can to disrupt it because if we catch them at the looking stage they will usually leave, so that is the best time to put them off. They will be looking for routines that they can exploit, so we will do things that break patterns in order to counter the results of their surveillance and avoid presenting them with a weakness. Our anti-surveillance measures will involve looking outside the perimeter to see what they are up to.

The second opportunity to deter them comes after their surveillance, when they try to break through that first line of defense. When we detect intruders at this point, we can illuminate or train cameras on them and use dogs to deter them from going into the residence. The risk of someone actually breaking in with guns, when we don't have any, is actually very slight. Even that can be offset at the surveillance stage. Although bodyguards carrying guns is illegal in the UK, there might be other ways to show someone that the target is not a soft touch. Shooting a troublesome fox on land that you own is legal. If you were carrying out surveillance on a place and you witnessed people doing that or shooting game, you might think twice about breaking into an estate with guns on it. The bodyguards might have no intention of using them against you but you won't know that for sure.

If a security team does spot an intruder and thinks they might be armed or just dangerous, the best option is to head for the safe room. When the police are called, possibly from inside the safe room, they will arrive within minutes and they are allowed to be armed. A lot of alarms go straight to the police, in fact. Let's say there is an average response time of nine minutes before an armed police unit arrives; that gives the criminals a very small window of opportunity between triggering that first perimeter alarm and getting out of the estate with whatever it is they came for, before they are taken down. During that short period of time, the criminals will come up against the obstacle of a virtually impregnable safe room and they won't be able to find a way in, no matter how tooled up they are.

If they take all of these measures, our couple of newly famous, high-net-worth individuals will be safe against any external threat.

FIGHT OR FLIGHT

The best way to keep a client safe is to prevent an attack. The simplest way to do that is to spot one coming before it happens, and I specialize in that. When you know the rules of the fight game as well as I do, it is easier. There is a certain pattern that you always have to abide by. The buildup to a fight or an attack is like a ladder going upwards and there are moments when you can choose to step off and away from that ladder.

The first thing to note is that there is always surveillance of some kind as part of victim selection. That is equally true even for seemingly random attacks from hostile drunks in pubs. A lot of victims think this did not happen to them before they were attacked, but when I talk them through the assault, they realize it did occur after all. At some point, they have been identified as a victim. It could be someone looking at them briefly from across the room or watching them for weeks, months or even years in extreme cases. That is how pedophiles groom their victims.

People who make a career out of violence are black belts at this kind of thing and most members of the public are white belts, so if you want to avoid being hurt, you have to up your game. If you can spot an assailant identifying a victim, and it is clearly you or your client, then you don't step on the ladder. You can avoid that by leaving a venue and just walking away. If I am out with the client, there is a rule of three. If I see a person three times, we leave that place. I don't have to ask why that person is there. I don't want to know why; I just leave.

If someone looks at me in the pub and they are not looking in a nice way, my choice is to either stay there or leave. If you choose to stay, it means you have accepted this risk to you. So now you are willingly standing on the first rung of the ladder.

If you are standing in the kebab shop at the end of the night and someone gives you a nudge or says something sarcastic to you, you are on the ladder because they have identified you as a victim. Now, if it is a kebab shop and I am on my own and I have had a few pints, I'd fancy my chances and I would probably stay but I would maneuver myself into a position where I could watch that person. If they moved any closer to me, I would bang them out. If I was with a client, the situation would be very different. If someone looks at the client, I would take them out of there straight away because ego does not play a part when you are a professional bodyguard. I have seen lots of bodyguards where their ego *has* played a part and, once it does, they are no longer playing the game professionally.

If you miss the victim selection phase, the next stage is the approach. If someone wants to attack you, they have to approach you. You have to get close to someone to kill them. This is particularly true if they are angry or jealous or mad about something and blaming it on you. They will probably want to say something and they have to get close enough to do that and then injure or kill their victim. This is why you see people jump up onto a stage with a pistol and press it right up against the head of someone. That weapon could kill from twenty meters, but when they are angry, they want to get close. It's not about the gun or its range, it's about them looking someone in the eye then killing them. Even professionals want to know they have killed someone, so they will need to be close enough to make sure that the job is done. When an attack happens, it is nearly always quite close, within a foot or so of the victim.

An approach can be very fast. It could happen when someone grabs you, turns you around and headbutts you, but it is not generally like that. Usually, an attacker has to work their way around to do this. If you spot the approach, you get out of there. Identifying the attacker is crucial. In a survey carried out on convicted street muggers, 90 percent of them said that if they are noticed by the victim before the attack, they stop there and then and choose another victim because they want an easy target, not a hard one.

If you miss the approach stage, you go up the ladder to another rung. The next stage is the interaction. Normally it's a verbal interaction, which could be a distraction or a threat.

You might be walking down the street and someone stops you and asks, "Have you got the time, mate?" so you look at your watch. If I was with you and I saw that, I would more than likely recognize it as part of the process of victim selection. I would make some room, because distance equals time, and I would say, "Sorry, I don't know; perhaps try in that shop over there." Or, if I thought an attack was imminent, I could shout, "Fucking back off!" I would be quite aggressive and make them go away.

Other types of distraction include asking questions like, "Haven't I seen you somewhere before?" Or something like,

"My mum knows your mum." This is designed to disarm your brain into thinking everything is okay and then comes the attack.

Once you understand what is happening, you can step off that ladder at any time but you have to be looking for it all the while. You can spot an attacker if you know the telltale indicators. There are clear signs of adrenaline before an attack. The body is getting ready for fight or flight, so it is putting all of its resources into the major muscles and cortisone is being released. This can result in pooling of the blood. Your hearing closes down and you get tunnel vision; your fine motor skills won't work anymore, so you get fidgety or twitchy, and your neck starts moving in an involuntary pecking motion, a bit like a chicken's. Sometimes, you can only say one-syllable words, which is why when two blokes in the pub are aggressively squaring up to one another, one of them will be going "Yeah? . . . Yeah?" and the other one is saying, "And? . . . And?" and they are pecking their heads toward each other while they are doing this.

Professional bodyguards look for signs of adrenaline all of the time. When they see a line of people in a queue waiting to shake hands with a celebrity, they look for indicators like someone constantly tapping their phone and not even looking at it. Because your fine motor skills stop working thanks to adrenaline, all of those elaborate self-defense skills they teach women, like taking an attacker's hands and twisting their wrists, don't work because they are too tricky when the adrenaline kicks in.

If you can identify an attacker at the bottom of the ladder and you knowingly take the risk of staying, your adrenaline creeps up, as you are thinking about the attack at that early level. By the time it then happens, you are ready for it; your adrenaline has gradually increased and you are in control of it, rather than it being in control of you; you don't experience an adrenaline dump that leaves you incapable of doing anything. You come back down and, bang, you can hit them. If you don't see an attack coming and that person hits you out of the blue, that massive and sudden adrenaline rush can be like the equivalent of sitting in your house calmly watching the telly one moment and an armed burglar suddenly bursting through your window the next. This can massively affect people's ability to respond to a threat. They can shit, piss, puke or just lie helpless on the floor. They might try and fight or run away but can't do anything with their hands, so that is the worst state to be in.

People sometimes wonder how I can know a person is genuinely aggressive but I am always looking for the signs of adrenaline leakage in their face. I check their eyes so I can see what they are looking at. I might even speak to them and ask, "Are you alright, mate?" to see if they can respond. If they don't answer me, I know their hearing has shut down. During an incident, the principal won't hear what you are saying to them either. There is no point saying, "Do this, do that, go here, go there." Because they simply cannot hear you. You have to drag them away. It's like a fighter when he is in the ring. He doesn't hear the crowd. He gets tunnel vision instead and all he can focus on is the opponent in front of him.

Distractions can be a physical act too. If I leaped out on someone and shouted at them then waved a knife in my left hand, they would look at the knife. I could then bang them out with the other hand and they wouldn't even see it coming. If I wanted to be sure of that, I could get vocal: "See this knife? I am going to fucking stab you in the face with it!" I guarantee they won't be able to take their eyes off the knife because that is the threat they would focus on.

217

Bodyguards will always do a stop check. If you come up to me aggressively, I will force myself to look to my left and right before I engage with you because I am looking to see who is with you. I do this because I know that if I don't, I will have tunnel vision at this point and I might not see accomplices or other threats, so I make myself do it. You occasionally see footage of members of Special Forces using a weapon; when they let off a couple of rounds, they look left then look right, then get their eyes back on the target again. They do that to make sure they never get blindsided.

If I walk into a pub as the close protection advance party, I will sit with a soft drink or a coffee, watching everyone in there for signs of adrenaline leakage. That person who looks like they might be a threat could be high on cocaine or they might have mental health issues but I don't care. I do not want to know why they are acting that way. I don't ask that question. I will simply tell the principal and other team members that there is something off about someone in that room, so don't come in here.

If there are a few of us and the possible assailant is just a lone person, a woman perhaps, we might agree that it is okay to come in after all but we would make sure we sit away from them and I will keep my eye on that person. All the team will now know that she is there, showing signs of adrenaline, and we will be watching her. If she gets up and walks toward the principal, we will assume this is the approach stage and someone will stand up straight away and intercept her. He might say "Excuse me, madam, can I help you?"

She might then explain herself by saying, "I was just going to the toilet," and our guy will point her away from us and send her on her way because we will have deliberately kept the principal away from the route to the toilet.

It is not just individuals who can lose their minds when adrenaline flows. Crowds can collectively do it too. I was looking after the Scottish rugby team at Twickenham in 2015, when they played their massive World Cup quarterfinal match against Australia. It ended in a highly controversial manner, with an incorrect decision from the referee, Craig Joubert, awarding a penalty to the Aussies in the dying seconds of the game. The Scots were on the verge of a historic win only to have it cruelly snatched from them. They lost by a single point and thousands in the crowd were very unhappy about that and soon made their feelings known.

The ref ran from the pitch at the final whistle and had to lock himself in his dressing room. Meanwhile, the Scottish team captain and manager had to go and do TV interviews in another building fifty yards away or face a massive fine but the crowd was between us and the studio and the fans were pissed off. It didn't matter that we were with the Scottish players and these were Scottish fans. The crowd was too big and aggressive and the players looked pretty scared when they started pulling and grabbing at them.

I took the Scottish team captain, Greig Laidlaw, while my mate took the manager, Vern Cotter. Laidlaw looked at the crowd and asked me, "Lee, do you think we will be okay?" I certainly hoped so.

I was lead bodyguard in an eight-man team as we tried to make it through. Ten or fifteen meters in, most of the crowd had realized the players and manager were there and they started pushing and crowding in. Ironically, my time as a former football hooligan helped me here because I know how crowds work and I can read them. I realized this crush was going to be a problem, so I looked at my mate and said, "Right, we are going to break out from the main security to get through. Get their heads down. We will send security one way and we are going the other." It was loud and there was a lot going on. I was shouting at the team leader that we had to go. She took a right, forty-five-degree turn and they started walking that way while we bust out to the left.

I shouted, "Grab on to me!" and everyone grabbed on to everyone else. I knew that the crowd was completely focused on the uniforms of the guys going the other way, so they didn't see us come out, even though we were very close to them. I had the captain underneath my right arm and I was pushing with my left hand as I made my way out. The crowd just split and let us through. They were trying to get past us, in order to reach Greig and Vern, because they didn't understand who we were or what was happening. They had collective tunnel vision so they no longer saw us. The crowd got thinner and thinner until eventually we pushed our way through and emerged out the other side.

PTSD

I was going to die and I knew it. I managed to get down on the floor and crawl on my belly but that was all I was capable of because my arms and legs would not work anymore. I knew I was a dead man and the only thing that mattered now was getting to my children so I could say goodbye. Then I was going to die.

It took all of my remaining strength to crawl to them. I don't remember much about it but I do recall that I managed to see Damon for the last time and kiss my sleeping little boy goodbye. Next, I crawled to the girls' room and made my peace with Chamane and Janine. Then I lay down on the floor and waited to die. I knew it was coming and accepted the fact. Then I died, in my head.

It must have been an hour later when I realized that perhaps I wasn't actually going to die after all, but that made no sense either. I had been so sure of it, so how come I was still lying there breathing? Eventually, I was able to get up and go downstairs, make a hot drink and think about what had just happened. I had woken in the night knowing with absolute certainty that I was about to die. I couldn't put a name to that feeling at the time but now I suppose I would call it a panic attack. A very severe one.

It was a horrible experience and the feeling stayed with me for days afterwards. Even then—and this was back in 1991—I realized it was probably linked to what I had seen and done in the military. But people knew a lot less about mental health then and rarely discussed PTSD, which I eventually realized was what I was suffering from.

Although I wouldn't recommend going through an experience like that to anybody, it did have one positive aspect. While sitting in my kitchen in the middle of the night, sipping my hot drink while my heart continued to beat, I realized that when I was lying there in the girls' room, I had reached a point where I had accepted my death. That robbed me of my fear of dying. It didn't mean that I wanted to die and I certainly didn't put myself in perilous situations deliberately afterwards. I didn't have a death wish and I wanted to carry on living but I did stay very calm when things started to get dangerous. I accepted that death could happen and was no longer frightened of it.

If you think that makes me a little odd, you are not alone. Back in 1999, when I started seeing Kate, she used to stay over in my cottage on the Al-Fayed estate in Scotland. After a few months, she said, "I would like to speak to you about something. I think you might have some issues."

"What do you mean?" I asked, completely oblivious.

"It's very disturbing sleeping with you at night," she told me. "It's like lying next to a wild animal." She explained that I would thrash around in bed, shout and even scream in the night. I was shocked because I wasn't aware of any of this and had no memory of it the next day.

Over the next few weeks, I started to understand that some of the strange stuff I did was possibly linked to post-traumatic stress. My granddad fought in Burma during the Second World War. When he came home again afterwards, he ran pubs in Manchester but he drank heavily and suffered massively from shell shock or what we would now call PTSD. It can affect anyone, no matter how tough they might think they are—and he was a very tough bloke. I realized I had been suffering with this for years. I had OCD, I was paranoid and sometimes I drank too much because my head was too "busy." I can normally cope with things like a car backfiring but don't ever ask me to go to a fireworks display. It's just too much for me.

I had been in Northern Ireland for two years. I'd seen friends get badly injured and killed. That stays with you. Certain times of the year were worse than others and I used to have some really dark days. On occasions, those days could turn into weeks. When things were really bad, I couldn't do anything and I didn't care anymore, even if it cost me my job. When it was like that, I could barely get out of bed. I spoke to friends who were military veterans about this and they understood. A few of my old mates had even killed themselves because of it.

Luckily for me, Kate was amazing and she decided not to run in the opposite direction. Not only did she put up with all of this strange behavior and support me, she did a lot of research into the subject to increase our knowledge of PTSD.

I suppose, looking back, I should not have been so surprised to learn that I had acted like this. When I worked on the Al-Fayed security team, we often had to sleep in reasonably close proximity to one another and I was regularly woken by one of the other guys going through the same thing. They would be noisily reliving their own personal traumas. The next morning, we might joke about it: "Bloody hell, mate, what were you doing last night? Who was that you were fighting in your sleep?" But if you weren't used to that kind of behavior, it could be disturbing.

A week or so before Princess Diana came to stay in St. Tropez, we got a delivery of some extra armored vehicles and supplies. The civilian guys who drove them over stayed in our accommodation at the villa, which consisted of some very nice rooms built underneath the tennis courts. One of the rooms had eight bunks in it, so the three drivers slept there that night, along with members of the security team. The next morning, I saw them at breakfast. They looked knackered and freaked out. I asked them what was wrong and one of them said, "It was terrifying. I thought one of your men was going to get out of bed and kill us in the night!" Whatever he had heard, he wasn't used to it and his mates felt the same way. Veterans can laugh that kind of thing off but these blokes were so freaked out that they found somewhere else to sleep the following night and refused to go back in with any of the security boys.

Fortunately for me, in 2004, I met an alternative healer, Goran Stall, and started training him for free. He became a black belt and, in return, he began treating me for my PTSD. After six months, he had changed my life. We talked and did therapy sessions. He taught me strategies for coping. He also used kinesiology, the study of body movement, to help me balance my body. Some of his ideas might have seemed a bit wacky at the time but they worked for me and that was the main thing. The easiest way to imagine it is to think that you can experience PTSD on a scale and that might move up or down between one and ten. Some days it is at one and manageable and on other, very bad days it is right up there at ten. Between 2004 and 2005, I had therapy and since then I would say it has been under control. I do still have bad days from time to time but generally I am doing fine.

Now I have very few bad episodes and am a lot better than I was, but I don't suppose I will ever be fully free of PTSD. A couple of years ago, I was sitting in the hot tub with Kate in our back garden when I heard a bang. That was all it took for my mind to switch into a mode of recognizing and analyzing a threat. I was working out the caliber of the gun and how far away the gunman was. On the second bang, I was convinced it was a shotgun; the assailant was thirty meters away and he was coming to get me. I leaped out of the hot tub naked and ran to a bush to wait there, so I could attack whoever was coming round the corner to kill me.

It took minutes for me to realize the truth. There was no gunman; no one was trying to kill me; it was probably just a car backfiring. I was standing naked in a bush and my wife probably thought I had gone completely mad. I walked sheepishly back to the hot tub.

"What the hell just happened?" Kate asked me.

I started to explain but settled on, "I've just been a dickhead."

Kate laughed and said, "You idiot."

THE TROUBLE WITH DAMON

I was the up-and-coming guy in the UK karate world in the eighties before I joined the Army. I had all the attributes and did the training but I couldn't follow it all the way to international recognition. I started the sport in my late teens but my son Damon grew up with martial arts and, from a very young age, he was hooked. He would watch videos of fights over and over. Once he started training with me, he took to it naturally and I realized he was exceptionally good at it. He was a kickboxer and I thought he had a real future in the sport.

It has been very challenging to coach Damon because we are so close. Sometimes it feels as if we are more like friends than father and son. Damon always had strong views on how things should be and, being a young fella, he tended to take the path of least resistance, but in martial arts you can't take shortcuts. It was a constant battle of wits, with me trying to include things he enjoyed while giving him a solid base of martial arts as his foundation.

I am incredibly proud of Damon. He is a very clever guy who has achieved so much in his sport, but it was hard not to give up on him at times. We had some challenging moments but perhaps that is why our relationship is stronger than ever now. For years, though, if Damon didn't want to do something, all I had to say to him was, "Shot put."

The shot put story shows the struggle we had to see each other's points of view in the early days. When Damon first came up to Scotland, the first sport he was really good at was the shot put. He beat everyone at his school then went to the county level and beat everyone there, too, so he was selected to put the shot in the north of Scotland championship in Inverness, with a view to getting on the national team.

I got a shot put and read up on the sport, then watched other guys training. I dug a sand pit at our place then tried to show him how to do it properly because his technique wasn't there. Damon's strength meant he reached good distances, but he wasn't loading up on his back leg and driving through with his hip and shoulder. I kept coaching him but he would not do it and this went on for weeks. He was ten years old and already stubborn as hell.

Damon was the smallest kid in his category at the event and he was very nervous. On the first go, everybody threw farther than him and they were all doing it properly.

At the last minute, Damon tried to change his style but panicked because he couldn't remember how. I told him it was fine to just do it his way and his last throw was a really good one. He even came second and the lad that beat him broke the north of Scotland national record by a foot and a half, so Damon had done very well. He picked up a medal but didn't get to represent the country and I think he really wanted that. We drove home without saying anything, but when we got back to the cottage, he went outside and did it exactly the way I had shown him. It was a massive throw—six feet farther than the winning one at the tournament and seven-and-a-half feet longer than the previous Scottish national record. I looked at Damon and he looked at me and we didn't say a fucking word.

For years afterwards, I think he resented it because he thought I was telling him that I was right and he was wrong and not just trying to help him improve, which was my intention. He finally got it in the end though. After that, if he was being a dick, I would just look at him and say, "Shot put."

And he would reply, "Okay, alright, I get it."

Damon didn't know anything about my martial arts history. I never discussed it in the house but I started to train him, once or twice a week, on a punch bag in the fishing room at the local pub. Damon learned well and soon got really into it. He would often train six times a week, even while he was still at school, but I never forced him to because I didn't want him to resent it. We did amateur kickboxing, which is lighter contact than pro kickboxing, a bit like the difference between amateur and pro boxing. You are not supposed to try and knock someone out; in fact, you get penalized if you do.

As Damon's coach, I tried to improve his game plan and increase his ability as an athlete. We had phases of training where we focused intensely on certain things. For example, we did two months of strength and conditioning training and plyometrics to increase muscle power and once spent another two solidly focusing on delivering one punch.

Damon is known as a hard hitter because he is technically excellent. When he hits, he knocks people down. I used to video Damon's footwork then measure his foot-travel on a move to within five millimeters then work until we could increase his projection by as much as a foot. Winning was important to Damon, but it wasn't everything to me. I wanted to improve him in the long run. Of course, I was his dad as well as his coach, and what does a dad know? Nothing, of course. To get Damon to do anything, I would have to tell him, then show him, then prove it to him.

For a long while, our life revolved around training. Even on holiday, we would take all our kit with us. If he wasn't training, Damon was watching videos over and over again so he could spot something to use in a tournament.

Damon had to maintain his weight, so all of his proteins, fats and carbohydrates needed to be balanced. He ate healthily at home all the time but he could eat what he wanted when he was out with his mates. Like most young men, he had a drink from time to time but training and good diet meant he could get away with it.

But the trouble with Damon was that he was great in the gym but when we put him in a tournament everyone used to beat him. It was so frustrating. He had the talent but there was obviously something preventing him from being as good as he should have been. I couldn't work it out at first.

Eventually, I realized the problem. He was scared of being hit, which is a bit of an occupational hazard for a kickboxer. So much so that when he was fourteen, he faked an injury at a tournament. "If you are faking this," I told him, "it's okay to walk away now." I could tell he wanted to because he was shit-scared, but technique- and skills-wise he was absolutely one of the best. He just lacked the nerve for the fight.

After that, I stopped Damon from competing for six months but he didn't want to give up the sport. He carried on and continued to fight in the club, where he beat everyone in our academy. It seemed that he didn't want to fight in tournaments but was well up for it on his home turf. It was a dilemma and we had to sort it out, but how? I decided to tackle the issue head-on.

I took my son into the gym, locked the doors and got him to put the gloves on. It was just the two of us. I got Damon to fight me and it was full-on. He was fifteen by now and a big lad, so he was punching and kicking me hard and pretty soon there was blood on my face.

When we finally stopped, I told him, "Look, Damon, you have not hurt me. See, it's just a bit of blood but I'm not really hurt. In a tournament you won't even be hitting or getting hit that hard because it's about connecting and scoring points not battering people, so there is no reason to be scared of it." I hoped Damon had learned that he could take some punishment in a fight and he would be fine.

There was a guy in his category called John Kirkwood who used to beat Damon every time. At the next tournament, Damon fought John in the team event and got his arse kicked. I was thinking my message hadn't sunk in after all. Then Damon fought John again in the individual category and absolutely annihilated him. When I watched that fight, I instantly knew two things. My son had finally realized there was no reason to be scared and he was going to be a world champion one day. He was that good. From that fight onwards, Damon was fine and soon he was international class.

Meanwhile, my junior team quickly became one of the best around. When I started my martial arts academy in Scotland, everyone told me it was too isolated and no one would come, but I was on a mission to prove them wrong. I studied coaching in depth and trained my guys like proper athletes, rather than recreational martial artists. Slowly and surely, we became one of the top teams in the UK then Europe. People started to notice when we fought the Bristol Death Squad, a team full of seasoned world champions. My team of sixteen-year-old boys gave them one hell of a shock. Our opponents won by a point after five bouts, but people started to really notice Damon that day when he fought Sean Viera, a triple world champion. He lost by a single point during an epic bout. Everybody was amazed because Damon was still only sixteen. Sean came up to me after the fight and said, "Where the fuck has he come from? He hit me so hard I thought, shit, I am going to have to do something quickly here or this kid is going to kill me." It was a massive fight for Damon and I knew then that he was going to be big.

Ironically, after telling Damon he couldn't get badly hurt in a contest, I ended up with a pretty serious injury that I sustained while we were putting on an exhibition match. I am obviously no stranger to pain, but considering the profession I am in and all of the sparring and fighting I have done over the years, I reckon I have been fairly lucky with injuries. I have had a few broken fingers and toes and some teeth knocked out. I have broken my ribs several times during karate and once on an Army assault course, when I broke three of them in one go, but I have never had anything from fighting that was as serious as that major injury back in my Army days, which put me in intensive care for three months on spinal traction.

My worst fighting injury was caused by Damon, though he didn't mean it. My boy had already knocked out two of my back teeth while sparring with me on a previous occasion. I had to have screw-in implants that cost me three grand a piece, so that was an expensive training session! The worst injury happened while we were doing a demo in front of a hundred people at a big event.

We planned what we were going to do and I told him, "When I put my guard down, you do the spinning jump kick." I was expecting an impact to the side of my head that I could lean into and I knew he wouldn't kick me too hard. When it came to the big moment, though, he must have panicked because instead of the spinning jump kick I was expecting, I got a massive punch in the face. Kate watched in horror and told me afterwards that she thought he had broken my neck.

Afterwards, I said, "Fucking hell, Damon, what the fuck?"

"I'm sorry, Dad, I didn't think I could make the kick."

He was only sixteen at the time but he could hit really hard and I wasn't expecting it, which heightened the blow. I couldn't move my neck for weeks and I needed whiplash treatment for fifteen years. The treatment would work for a while and I would be able to train, which would then set it off again. I needed to carry on competing and sparring, but doctors warned me that this injury could be a big one and might have a serious impact on my life. After my last world championships, when I won the silver medal, I decided enough was enough, so I stopped sparring. It has been four years since I have been hit by anyone and there has been no more neck trauma so hopefully it's sorted.

When Damon left school, he chose Nottingham University so he could carry on with his kickboxing there, coached by Owen King, a former world champion. During his three years at uni, I spoke to Damon nearly every day on the phone. He went out on the piss and had a fantastic time but still trained every week with Owen—a good coach who brought a new dimension to Damon's fight plan. He taught Damon a more defensive style of fighting, which I didn't like at first but I have to admit it worked and he helped Damon to win a British World Association of Kickboxing Organizations (WAKO) Championship.

After college, I arranged a couple of fights for Damon in Sicily where he won a world championship fight, but the icing on the cake was going to the WAKO World Cup in Italy and winning there too. I thought, *This kid has really got it.*

Damon was a member of the British WAKO team when they were crowned world champions for the first time ever and he fought brilliantly. His progress was incredible, but kickboxing is still an amateur sport and we always knew there was a limit to what he could achieve in it. Then we heard that the British taekwondo team had made a decision to cast their net wider and look for fighters from different martial arts codes through their Fighting Chance program. Damon decided to give it a go, attending a series of boot camps and getting on the team. This was a step up because now he was being trained as an Olympic athlete. Damon soon became one of the fittest guys there but, because he was an outsider, no one knew who he was. No one liked him either, including referees and officials, because he had come from kickboxing. It was like a rugby union player going to play rugby league or vice versa.

Damon kept going but it was an uphill battle and he still talked about kickboxing all the time. It came to a head when he called me in tears after a tournament in Barcelona. He was twenty-three years old, he had just lost and felt he really couldn't do this new sport anymore because the pressure and expectation on him was too high. I told him to fly back home so we could talk about it.

I let Damon speak about all the pressures and the difficulties he had encountered as well as the hostility. I heard him out then

I said, "Listen, Damon, this is the score. I hear everything you are saying but now I am going to lay it out for you." Then I told him, "How dare you not fully commit to this sport when taxpayers are paying you actual money to do this. You get to use all of these excellent facilities and you are doing something that most people can only dream of. How dare you take their money and not show up. Now, you have two options: you either sort your shit out or you leave the program. If you stay, you can actually make a difference to people you have never met and possibly inspire them but, right now, you are not showing up. There are kids in the military in Afghanistan who are younger than you and they are dying over there. That's real pressure. You either commit one hundred percent to this or you tell them you are quitting."

It was an emotional moment for both of us. He was crying and we were hugging and I told him, "No one else will tell you this, only I can do it and you can tell me to fuck off if you like, but that doesn't matter because I love you."

After that, Damon stepped up to the mark, put his doubts to one side and gave everything. He started winning and he didn't stop. Damon won big competitions, beating top names in the taekwondo world. In 2015, he went to the world championships in Russia and won the silver medal for Great Britain.

A year later, it seemed certain he would be selected for the 2016 Rio Olympics. Damon was ranked fourth in the world by then and was the world championship silver medalist, so it looked like there was no way he could be ignored by the selectors, but in the end Lutalo Muhammad was chosen instead. Damon was devastated at narrowly missing out and it knocked the stuffing out of him.

He didn't quit though. Damon trained hard for another two years but had a big injury setback, which left him on crutches, then he had his shoulder reconstructed too. Just a few months later, he went to the 2017 world championships in South Korea and won the bronze medal, while still on his way back from injury.

Damon knew he was too old for the next Olympics and retired from taekwondo as the only British male athlete to win two consecutive medals at the world championships. He is one of the top people in the world in his sport with a massive following and so many people love him. I am incredibly proud of my son and all of his achievements in the sport. We are very close after everything he has been through because we were with him every step of the way.

We were always fully committed to helping Damon to succeed. We drove tens of thousands of miles each year getting him to tournaments all over the UK and Europe. We stayed in a lot of hotels and I tried to sponsor kids on the team who couldn't afford that themselves, so it was not a cheap undertaking. Kate and I decided to have no birthday or Christmas presents one year because we had spent £18,000 on travel and could not afford them, but we knew it was important for Damon to keep his momentum.

We would have done this for any of my kids, but he was the one most interested in pursuing it. Both of my girls could have reached the same standard as Damon, but after staying with us for a couple of years, they wanted to go back to Blackpool. Damon carried on and I am so glad he did because we have had some amazing moments. Aside from watching him win his world championship medals, the best day was when we fought alongside each other at the WUMA (World United Martial Arts) European Kickboxing Championships in Cheltenham, in 2008. I was fighting in my category on the next mat to Damon and we both won gold medals. That was definitely one of the highlights of my life.

When I watch Damon fight, I throw every punch and kick and I can feel every blow that lands on him. We share the ups and downs, the sadness and the elation and I could talk you through a lot of his old fights blow by blow, even now.

The biggest fights Damon had were in taekwondo. Winning the silver medal in the world championship was amazing and his fight in the semi-final, when he beat Aaron Cook on a golden point at the end, was just incredible. He fought some of the best fights he has ever had to get his medal. He was magnificent when he won bronze too. Damon switched to a new code at a late age and had to learn a lot to excel at it. The level he reached in the sport put him in the same tier of funding as Mo Farah and it doesn't get much more elite than that!

DAD

Damon's Story

"When I was a boy of fourteen, my father was so ignorant I could hardly stand to have the old man around. But when I got to be twenty-one, I was astonished at how much he had learned in seven years." That Mark Twain quote probably sums up the way I felt about my dad when I was younger. We got on very well but I did not always appreciate or listen to the advice he gave me and would sometimes try to do things my own way when I should have listened to him instead. He will never let me forget that shot put story!

I eventually realized that Dad knew a great deal and he was always there to pass that knowledge on to me. That is not to say we agree on everything and he can get a bit obsessive about things. I don't think other people's fathers lectured their sons about the right way to climb into a car, for example: "You should go in leg first for safety, not duck your head in." He would tell me but then he would make me do it properly . . . again and again. I would have to climb into the car his way ten times or more before he was finally satisfied and we could drive away. He has that slightly obsessive, military-bodyguard mindset and extreme attention to detail that can seem a bit odd to civilians, especially a ten-year-old.

Now I look back on times when I had thought he was being a bit harsh on me but I realize that it was always for my benefit, not his. Dad never judges you and he doesn't have an ego. He just wants you to fulfil your potential.

Before he came to collect me, I was living with my sisters and mum and, like any boy, I was probably trying to be an alpha male but I was a bit too young for that role. I think my mum realized I needed a male influence in my life and fair play to her for making such a selfless decision and letting me go all the way to the Highlands of Scotland with Dad. I can remember sitting high up in the seat of the van he hired to move his stuff. I must have asked him, "Are we there yet?" every two minutes for the nine hours it took us to get to our new home. I was quite excited about this new life and looking forward to spending time with my dad. Prior to this, I tended to see him every few weekends because he was away a lot. I was aware of what he did for a living and it was the coolest thing to tell people—"My dad is a bodyguard"—but he didn't really talk about it. He is a quiet and humble man and I didn't realize how good he was at martial arts, even when he started training me. Dad is the type of bloke who goes to a party and comes away knowing everything about everyone else without telling anyone much about himself. I am the same, to be honest.

I had a brilliant childhood and it was amazing to be taught so many things at such a young age. It was so cool to come home from school and jump on a quad bike or drive to the loch and go fishing or shooting but Dad would make sure I knew all the safety drills and we were never reckless.

It was great having Kate as a stepmum too. She is a very wise person and has always been there for me throughout my life. When I needed someone to talk to and confide in, other than Dad, she was ideal. He was away when I decided to retire from competitive taekwondo and it was Kate I talked to about that before making my final decision. I suppose there were times when she was trapped in the middle, between two alpha males butting heads, but that is probably the case in a lot of households and she has been brilliant for both of us.

I started martial arts training at twelve, which is quite late. Most members of the national team started at four or five. At fourteen, I was tall and the fights were set up based on height, not age, so I was often fighting against sixteen-year-olds. I was technically very good and the best in our club but I found it tougher to adapt to the stress of tournament combat. I spent ages trying to work out why I was getting nervous and frightened. The best fighters are the most aggressive and I could do that in the club but then I'd freeze at a tournament. It took me a while to realize that it was my adrenaline, which was triggering my flight and not fight response. Dad needed to show me I was not going to get hurt, which led to that momentous day in the gym where he encouraged us to really go at each other. Some people told him he shouldn't do it and he was kicking me pretty hard, to the point where I was in tears, but he told me afterwards, "Damon, I haven't really hurt you and you haven't really hurt me. If *I* can't hurt you, then those other guys definitely can't hurt you."

It finally clicked with me at that tournament not long afterwards, when I beat my big rival John Kirkwood, but it wasn't just my dad's encouragement that got me there. I used the satellite technique, where you imagine you are looking down on the earth as if from a satellite, then you realize that what you are about to do is not such a big deal in the context of everything else going on in the world. I managed to rationalize it by telling myself, "You can't die, so why are you getting yourself so worked up?" Yes, there is pressure but it is also an opportunity to do something, so you might as well enjoy yourself. Dad uses similar techniques in stressful situations and it works for him too.

I won lots of kickboxing events but the sport was tough on my shoulder, which subluxated more than twenty times. This is a partial dislocation and it would slip back in on its own but it was painful and I couldn't seem to find a way to prevent it from happening. It was Dad who suggested switching codes to taekwondo. Not only did it give me the chance to train as an Olympic athlete but it was better for my shoulder because 95 percent of taekwondo is kicks and not punches. In fact, you are not even allowed to punch to the head.

The first boot camp I attended had 1,500 applicants for the Fighting Chance program, with just three or four of us selected at the end. I had to fight someone in taekwondo rules for the first time and I won my opening bout against an Olympic taekwondo practitioner. My strength as a fighter is using my brain to absorb new things and I had learned the kicks obsessively. I fought the karate and taekwondo world champions and did well enough to be selected.

I have had highs and lows in the sport and Dad shared them with me. Winning a silver medal at the world championship in Russia in 2015 was a high point. Narrowly missing out on the GB Olympic team a year later was a very low one. Like Dad, I am a resilient person and I managed to come back from that dis-appointment to fight in the 2017 world championship in South Korea. I had to have two hip operations, left and right, before the championships and I shouldn't have come back so quickly but

I really wanted to fight in the homeland of the sport. I had just returned to proper training, with just six weeks left to prepare, when I injured my hand. They say these things come in threes!

Despite nursing that bad injury, I managed to ignore a lot of pain, train hard, fight well and win the bronze medal. As soon as I got home, I had an operation to repair a snapped tendon in my thumb. After all of the injuries, winning bronze there was probably a bigger achievement than my silver medal two years earlier.

Dad and I are quite similar. If I get into something, I want to know everything about it and he is the same. I would say we are both confident but humble people and we share a passion for combat sports. Now that I have retired from taekwondo, I have decided to get back into kickboxing because I miss competition. Martial arts is a big part of my relationship with my dad. It made us close, but we could also really fall out over it, too, at times and I am glad we have gone beyond that.

My dad has been my coach, my father and my best friend rolled into one and we still speak every day. He is a source of advice still but now, as I get older, I can occasionally point him in the right direction too. We have a special relationship with no secrets. Dad can say things to me that other people can't and he will give it to me straight. Before I applied myself fully to my sport, I was not living up to my potential. We had some harsh conversations about that but sometimes you need a rocket up your arse and, fortunately for me, my dad loved me enough to provide one when I really needed it. I wouldn't be the man I am today without my dad.

PROOF OF LIFE

Kate's Story

I was not looking for love on the day I first met Lee at the airport. I'd borrowed the college pool car to attend a meeting, then I went to pick up my parents from the same flight Lee was waiting for. The delayed plane was not good. I was supposed to be back at work and I was worried the pool car would be clamped, then I would have some explaining to do.

I hadn't even noticed Lee until I was in the queue for a coffee. I saw this impressively muscular forearm reach out in front of me to get something and I thought, *Who owns a forearm like that?* I followed that forearm with my eyes and was even more impressed. I think he must have felt my eyes boring into him because he looked back at me. Once we had our coffees in hand, I asked him if he knew why the plane was delayed and we got talking.

My parents were the first people to get off the plane. I had moved back home at the age of thirty and my overprotective father saw me chatting to this big bloke and he glowered. Lee was the first man with a tattoo that I had ever met and he has a certain aura. You always notice him when he walks into the room and my dad must have wondered who the hell he was.

A couple of weeks passed and by then I had placed Lee in the "what-might-have-been" file. I happened to be in the mail room at work when a card with my name on it suddenly arrived. I was so gobsmacked that a woman I worked with asked if I was okay. When I told her about this mysterious man at the airport, Lee quickly became the talk of the office. He thinks he called me up but Lee actually asked me to phone him and he had put his phone number on the card. It took me twenty-four hours to summon up the nerve and I must have dialed eight times before I let it actually ring. This man gave me the serious collywobbles and, if I am honest about it, he still does.

Once we started talking, it broke the ice and we couldn't stop. Lee mentioned he was coming up to see his cousin for a coffee and he asked me out. I was really attracted to him but we went on three dates before he gave me a kiss and I started to worry that he didn't really fancy me. He always drove and we would park at the bottom of Mum and Dad's driveway, out of sight, and he would say, "Night, then," and I would go in. I think he was being an old-fashioned gentleman but also not wanting to rush things because we could both sense that this was right. When he did finally kiss me, it was worth the wait.

I had never met anyone who was as modest as Lee. The man has no ego. He didn't even tell me he was a bodyguard and just talked vaguely about "looking after an estate." Because he lived on one, in "Keepers Cottage," and appeared to be taking care of it, I thought he was a gamekeeper. We had been going out for six weeks before I realized he was actually a bodyguard. Lee is a fighter but you wouldn't know it. Away from that world, he is the gentlest man you could imagine. We don't even row. Our oldest son, who is sixteen, has only ever heard us raise our voices to each other once and he was quite shocked by it.

When we drove back from Manchester airport following our holiday in Ibiza, I was glum because we lived ninety minutes apart but I didn't know how we could fix it. Lee felt the same. "I know exactly what we are going to do," he said. Lee resigned from his job, then he and Damon came up to live with me in my new flat. At the time, this did not seem to be an irresponsible thing to do. I just assumed we could make it work.

The first time I met Chamane, Janine and Damon, there were four teenagers all staying in Lee's cottage following a family reunion and it was pretty full-on. I got to know Damon pretty quickly and we had such a special relationship. I couldn't have kids and, up till that point, hadn't wanted children of my own as I just couldn't see what the benefits were. When I saw how much pleasure there was in spending time with Damon and how lovely it was to have a smaller version of Lee there, it completely changed my mind. We had only been together for two months when Lee told me, "I can't wait to have kids with you." I got really tearful when I explained that it wasn't an option. I was worried it would be over between us but he was really good about it. If kids weren't for us then we would just have to have a different life, without them. Years later, we were able to go down the IVF route, and though it took a long while and was a tremendously difficult process, it was so worth it in the end.

I "inherited" Damon when he was ten and soon attended my first parents' evening, which was a bit nerve-racking, particularly when I felt defensive if a teacher was critical of him. There are some advantages to being a fake-mum though. I taught him to do his own laundry by the age of fifteen. "I'm not your real mum, so I shouldn't have to be doing this for you," I said and he bought that.

Lee never quite got round to proposing to me, so I decided I would have to do it instead. It was a leap year and we were at the world championships in Vienna, as our lives revolved around martial arts competitions, so I decided to propose to Lee there. Damon was supposed to hold the video camera to capture the moment but he was desperate to watch a big fight instead, so there was no footage of Lee saying yes to me, but both Damon and I have happy memories of the day.

I always kept the books for our business so I knew we were taking a gamble when I stepped back to have Theo in 2004, but I hoped we had everything in place. We had been through our tenth round of IVF, which was a massive financial strain at £2,000 a time but Lee never gave up on me. We were heartbroken every time it failed but when it finally worked, we called our firstborn Theodore, which is Greek for "a gift from God."

I wanted to have time with my child but I realize now that I took my eye off the ball at exactly the wrong time. When the business crashed, it was awful. I was pregnant with the twins while people were trying to take the studio off us. I had a huge panic attack and ended up in the hospital. The lives of our babies were in danger and it was extremely traumatic.

We live in a small town and Lee was often away. I was left with the babies and everyone was asking if we were going to survive the sequestration process. I really struggled with that. I believe everything happens for a reason, though. I have managed to forgive everyone who I felt let us down and I have moved on but it was traumatic and brought back painful memories as I had been through this before.

I grew up in a posh part of Cheshire. We had money and owned a big house with a swimming pool, a croquet lawn and there were donkeys in a paddock. We had skiing holidays and my father was a member of the golf club. He was one of a dozen entrepreneurs to be invited to a Downing Street event when Margaret Thatcher was prime minister and won the Queen's Award for export. For his birthday, we had a marquee on the lawn for two hundred guests. It sounds great but everyone around cared far too much about money.

When the textile industry tanked, my dad lost everything overnight. My mother had to start working as a waitress and the restaurant let me work there, too, even though I was only fourteen. I would hand over the money I earned to her because we needed it for food. On my father's next birthday, no one came over. You certainly find out who your friends are when you lose all of your money.

My brother generously paid my school fees so I could stay on at St. Hilary's School for young ladies, but we didn't have enough money for the uniform. I looked a bit of a scruff, and girls at that age are hideously cruel.

Father worked with the receiver to pay off as many debts as possible and the administrator suggested he played golf with a businessman he knew. That guy was impressed enough to give my father a chance: "I am going to give you £10,000 to go to Hong Kong and find something we can import that this country needs. You have two months to set it up. Off you go."

My father always discussed business at our dinner table, so we helped guide him. Aerobics was massive at the time but you couldn't get the gear to wear for it, so he started the first mail order catalogue for leotards and leg warmers. It went so well he was asked to become MD of other companies in the same group until he was CEO and took the business public. It took my dad only four years from the point when he lost everything before he made it all back again. I knew that if he could do it, Lee and I could too. We were a team, a proper partnership, and always had been. We would just have to start all over again.

Between us, we earned just enough money to keep up payments on the house but he was away for two weeks at a time, training bodyguards. We had been together for a decade and were at rock bottom but we got on with it.

It seemed our financial problems might never end, so Lee looked at more dangerous jobs abroad, but he always downplayed the risks. He would pick his moment and say, "There is a really good job that has come up. Do you want to talk about it in the hot tub?" As if we were discussing a holiday and not Lee risking his life in an unstable country.

Before Lee left for Somalia, he changed before my eyes and became a different person. I could see him begin to distance himself from us because he was so focused on the job. He would open the door differently and even sit differently and then there was his packing list, which he began from scratch. We spent hours trying to find desert boots that had to go up to his ankles. I didn't understand why until that poor man was bitten by a carpet viper. We had to research the armor plating in bulletproof vests and Lee wasn't happy with the over-the-shoulder bags available because they were the wrong way round if he needed to pull out his Glock. I realized this was far more dangerous work than I was expecting.

If all of that weren't worrying enough, we had to go through "proof of life" documents in case he was kidnapped or captured by jihadists. To be able to prove that Lee was still alive, in case of a ransom demand or a rescue operation, the same company needed information that only he and I could possibly know. That included very personal things that could be turned into code words, like the name of our first dog or the place where we met.

I became very emotional. This was not what I signed up for but Lee felt he had to do it for financial reasons and wouldn't back out because he had made a commitment and that was that.

Somalia was bad enough but Libya was worse. He managed to get through to me from the compound and I could hear birds reacting to loud bangs. "I am struggling to hear you," I said. "Is that thunder?" Then I realized it was actually rockets landing close by.

I was just about to take the boys to school when Lee called and said, "We have to leave the camp now. This is just a quick call to say that I love you very much and the next time we speak I will hopefully be in a hotel lobby in Tunisia." I barely got to say anything back to him before he had to go. Then there was no word from him for fourteen hours. They were the worst hours of my life.

There was no one I could call to ask if he was okay. By lunchtime, I was trying to work out where he might be in Libya. When I picked up the boys from school I didn't say anything to them about Daddy coming home because I had heard nothing from him.

That night, I had to go to a surprise fancy dress party, so I took the boys to their Nanny Norma and got dressed for it. There I was, fretting like crazy about Lee and I was going off to a party dressed as a frigging cowgirl. I had to plant a smile on my face and I looked like a bloody line dancer.

I was still at the party when the phone finally rang. It was Lee but I couldn't hear him because the signal was so bad. I took the phone into a spare room and I had to stick my head out of the window in order to hear his voice clearly. I must have looked pretty peculiar but I didn't care. When he told me he had made it out of Libya safely, the relief was overwhelming. I started sobbing as soon as I heard his voice, then he told me he was flying home. I fell to bits when I came out and had to explain to everyone at the party that this was the call I had been waiting for and Lee was safe. I drove for four and a half hours to pick him up at Edinburgh airport and it was a very emotional reunion.

I realized early on that there was something wrong with Lee. Sleeping next to him was hideous and I had never heard sounds like it. There were screams and growls and I had to get out of the way when he lashed out in his sleep. I used to ask lots of questions about his PTSD at the beginning. It was new territory for me and I was finding my way through it. My naivety helped him open up because he knew it came from a place of love, with no judgment. I was in my flat the first time he called me to tell me he was struggling. "I am having a really bad night," he said and even his voice sounded different. It was like talking to a stranger. The memory of that little boy in Germany, held at knifepoint by his father, while Lee pointed a gun at the man, had triggered him that time. The boy and his father both survived but the stress of that incident stayed with Lee.

PTSD has affected Lee regularly over the years. When he goes to his dark place now, I can recognize the triggers. November is a difficult month because of Remembrance Day but there have been occasions when his bad spells have lasted all the way up till Christmas. Like depression, PTSD is such a personal journey. A friend dying can trigger it, or even talking to someone who is feeling the same way. When Lee starts to go, it is like he is stepping out of our happy household and walking away down a dark corridor. I tell the kids, "Daddy is going to a sad place."

And they understand. They saw him cry on Remembrance Day when they were young and it was upsetting but I told them it is okay for men to cry.

I have tried to give Lee a warm, safe place to feel whatever he needs to feel at any point. The PTSD might always be there but it doesn't dominate his life. When it hits him, it is a bit like throwing a jigsaw up into the air then having to patiently fit all of the pieces back in place, but we do that together.

I was relieved when Lee started working in safer countries and I refuse to let him go to war zones again. He has business partners now who recognize his management and leadership skills. His first contract in Saudi Arabia meant he was away for twelve weeks but at least he was safe and we were able to afford our first family holiday in years after that. Now things are going really well for us but it has been a difficult journey at times.

Lee is an amazing man and a great husband and father too. He speaks to his kids every day, either in person or on the phone, and it's always to talk about their lives and what they need. Everyone in our family knows he is there for them in a crisis and he is never judgmental. Lee will always come up with a strategy to help them but he will say, "This is just my advice. You don't have to take it." My husband is always the calm, no matter what the storm. It's one of the many things I love about him.

AFTERWORD—STILL FIGHTING

What makes a good bodyguard? Lots of things. Not everyone can do it or would want to because everything about it becomes a way of life. A bodyguard never switches off, whether on duty or off. You can't stop being vigilant when it is an important part of your life. You stay alert twenty-four seven. It can be obsessive.

Kate noticed this when I first met her. If we went to the pub for a drink, I would always check it out as we were walking in and work out where I wanted to sit to ensure we weren't vulnerable. I wanted a spot where I could see everything and everyone. I would know where all of the exits were. It was just instinct. There were times when we would leave a place even if we hadn't finished our drinks because I didn't like the feel of it, though I couldn't always explain the reasons why. It's what some people call a sixth sense. You feel the hairs on the back of your neck stand up. When I feel this, I trust it and I go to condition red. The adrenaline starts to do its job and I am ready for combat, checking everyone, working out who is a threat to me and formulating the best plan to deal with that threat.

I am not the only one who thinks like this. When I am in a pub with other members of the profession, we all have similar outlooks because of our experiences and training and we can spot a threat a mile off. Within minutes, someone would see something that didn't look right and he would say, "That guy over there, at your eleven o'clock; the one with the brown hair, wearing the blue T-shirt, drinking the orange juice," meaning he might be dodgy and we would have to keep an eye on him. It becomes second nature because it is ingrained in us to always look for that threat.

It is one thing to be able to spot a threat and another to have the will to deal with it, ruthlessly if need be. If you have to strike someone to neutralize an immediate, dangerous threat that they are presenting, you can't worry about the possible consequences or you won't do it right and they will still be a danger to you. You cannot hesitate or think about hitting a man too hard or the possibility that he might fall and die. If you have any problem worrying about the consequences of your actions, then you are in the wrong profession.

If I am in a public place and you do something that might affect my life or my client's, I will deal with you in a way that will render you unconscious and, if you fall and hit your head and die, then tough. I would be able to justify my actions in court because every person has a basic human right to defend themselves. If you are behaving in a threatening manner; if I believe you are going to do something to me and I have no other option available to me, I have a right to do that first. I am an expert when it comes to studying the psychology of an attack. "This is what I saw in his face," I would say, "so I had no option."

The way a human body reacts before an attack is always the same. The effects of adrenaline cause signs and indicators that can mean an assault is imminent. It's a bit like watching a lion on the Serengeti plain pick a victim then chase it down. I know how to mask those signs in myself so you won't know about it before I strike because I will not be showing the usual indicators of aggression. You won't even see me coming.

People talk about using reasonable force and of course you are not going to deliberately beat someone to death, but you also don't have to defend yourself "a bit"; you have to defend yourself fully and, if you are doing it right, the other guy is probably going to get hurt in the process. The idea is to get rid of the threat and move away to a place of safety. If I am going to effectively protect my client then I need to put you down quickly. If I don't and I end up in a protracted fight with you, then who is looking after my client at this point? No one. You might have someone with you who could take him or me down, so I can't waste time trading blows.

If you do have to deck someone then it is a good idea to hit them with an open hand. Most people don't realize that you can hit someone really hard like that, harder than a punch. Also, if I punch someone in the face, I could break a hand doing it and that could be catastrophic for me. I might not be able to drive or use my weapon and would be left with the use of only one hand. So hit with a palm, hit hard and never worry about the consequences.

It is the same principle if you have to shoot someone. I can't shoot you a bit. I will shoot you a lot. By that stage, I will have no choice because you are an imminent danger to me or the person I am guarding. If it is a case of you or us, believe me, it is going to be you.

So, aside from being ruthless and obsessive, what else does a bodyguard need to be? The next thing on my list is flexible. If you are the kind of person who has to stick rigidly to a plan without wavering then you won't be an effective bodyguard.

I ran a training exercise with a group of bodyguards, and after it, one of them said, "God, you fucked us about today." I had them working to a pre-planned routine then I threw in some changes to the route and schedule as we went along and forced them to react to events. I did that deliberately because it mirrors real life. When you are looking after high-level businessmen or celebrities, you can be sure they will want to make changes to their plans so you had better be ready for that eventuality. Normal people are just the same when you think about it. People generally don't want to be held to a rigid plan every day, so their bodyguards have to be flexible too.

Things have a habit of changing, no matter how carefully you plan, and it is not always the client's fault. In St. Tropez, we were due to pick up Princess Diana at a prearranged place and had some time to wait, so we set up on the beach and put the five vehicles we were in out of the way. Then the boat was delayed, so we ended up waiting there for ages but we were relaxed and killed time drinking mocktails until we were finally in contact with the boat, which confirmed the princess was twenty minutes away. I went to check the vehicles and was horrified to find that someone had put a big steel barrier across the road without us knowing, trapping us there. We had seen this old gate on the way in but it was open and looked like it hadn't been closed in a while. It turned out it was still in use. Shit, we couldn't get through and were about to be severely embarrassed if the princess arrived to find us all trapped on the beach and unable to move.

Then I spotted a bin lorry and ran after it, shouting at the driver to stop and come back. Luckily for us, he did and, even more fortunately, he had a key that fitted the gate because it was a municipal lock, so he was able to open the barrier and let us out, which spared us from humiliation.

The level of flexibility you have to display will depend on the individual client and your ability to influence them. They are the boss—they have hired you but are paying for your expertise—so you need to be able to tell them if they are about to put themselves in danger. A bodyguard can influence a client and will certainly advise against doing something risky. You can say, "Look, this is a dangerous place to be. My advice is don't go." More often than not, they will listen to you because they don't want to be killed. If they are stubborn or just don't like to be told "no" by anybody then they could insist on heading there anyway. That leaves you with a dilemma. You can either go with them or abandon them and they go on their own without protection. Personally, there is no way I would leave them. I might get home afterwards and resign and never work for them again but I will stick with them and make sure they get home safely first. You are contracted to the client for their protection and you cannot let them down.

That way of thinking obviously puts me at risk as well as the client but I have spent my life in harm's way to protect others. Somehow, I have survived incredibly dangerous situations in three war zones and lived to talk about them afterwards. I have been able to pass on my skills and experience, as both a bodyguard and a martial arts expert, to new generations, including my own son Damon, who became a world champion. A life spent dedicated to martial arts has given me the skills and experience to attain the level of eighth dan in karate, which is pretty rare in the UK.

The discipline of martial arts has helped me to stay resilient when things were not going well for us. My wife, Kate, and I managed to build a successful business from scratch then watched helplessly as it was cruelly taken from us almost overnight, thanks to a world economic crisis. That was quite possibly the worst time of what has often been a stressful and, I have to admit, hazardous life. I am proud that we did not buckle under the huge strain but instead kept going and started all over again. It took a while and was difficult but our business is now thriving once more. I now oversee major contracts providing close protection services all over the globe.

My martial arts school is going really well too. When I work with kids, we teach them military-values martial arts, so it is not just about combat or competing, it also instills the right values in them. I am passionate about this because it has helped me so much in my own life. We want to do this all over the country. I will still do some security work, but what I really want is to spend more time working with kids and teachers in the community and leave a legacy.

I am a lucky man with a fantastic family and I am involved in work that I love. Not many people get to say that. The modern world is a dangerous place and it always will be, so I am unlikely to be out of a job in the near future. Men with skills like mine will always be in demand somewhere but that's okay because I am still here and I am still fighting.

Lee Sansum, 2022

ACKNOWLEDGMENTS

I have been blessed to have had so many great role models in my life and to have gained so many friends along the way. I was lucky to meet those who challenged me, too, and made me the man I am today.

Many of those who helped me write this book are still operational and contribute to the safety of others around the world every day, so I can't name all of my brothers and sisters here, but you know who you are. I think of you all frequently, especially those who are no longer with us. God bless you all.

My dad was a gentle and loving man who taught me lessons I finally understood in later life. He was a good man. To my mum; brother, Brant; and sister, Lois, I have fond memories of growing up with you, as part of the Rossendale gang, and sharing some great adventures with all of our good friends.

Special thanks to my martial arts family, who are scattered around the world. Thank you to the athletes and coaches who taught me how to pass on the amazing life skills that the arts taught me.

I miss my Army pals from Sennelager, Catterick, Chichester, Tidworth, Hong Kong, Donnington and Northern Ireland, who made my years serving in the armed forces an absolute honor.

The crazy contractor crews in the UK, Libya, Somalia, Nigeria and Saudi Arabia are all amazing, and the work they do, protecting those at risk, under the most difficult conditions, is awesome. I miss you all daily. Stay safe out there.

Howard Linskey: thank you for taking the time to listen to me and, more importantly, to appreciate my vision for this book. Your enthusiasm, diligence and expertise are second to none. You made writing this book so easy. Thanks, mate.

Phil Patterson, my literary agent from Marjacq Scripts, is an extremely professional and super-cool guy, with stacks of enthusiasm, who looked after me every step of the way. Thanks for introducing me to the amazing Anna Valentine, at Orion, who shared your enthusiasm for this book, and the brilliant Shyam Kumar, who pulled it all together with his super team. Thanks, Phil, Anna, Shyam and the incredible crew at Orion, for publishing the book.

Kate, my love, you have been my rock throughout the writing of this book, as always. We shared the laughs and tears that those memories brought to the surface, which gave me time to reflect and just be in the moment. I adore you, lovely lady x

ABOUT THE AUTHOR

LEE SANSUM is an ex–Royal Military policeman, martial arts champion, private military contractor and expert in close protection. He has worked with Hollywood stars Tom Cruise, Nicole Kidman and Sylvester Stallone, as well as the legendary footballer Pelé. Working for the controversial billionaire Mohamed Al-Fayed, Lee went on to protect the most famous woman in the world, Princess Diana, with whom he formed a close bond.